New Approaches to E-Reserve

CHANDOS
INFORMATION PROFESSIONAL SERIES

Series Editor: Ruth Rikowski
(e-mail: Rikowskigr@aol.com)

Chandos' new series of books are aimed at the busy information professional. They have been specially commissioned to provide the reader with an authoritative view of current thinking. They are designed to provide easy-to-read and (most importantly) practical coverage of topics that are of interest to librarians and other information professionals. If you would like a full listing of current and forthcoming titles, please visit our web site www.chandospublishing.com or email info@chandospublishing.com or telephone +44 (0) 1223 891358.

New authors: we are always pleased to receive ideas for new titles; if you would like to write a book for Chandos, please contact Dr Glyn Jones on email gjones@chandospublishing.com or telephone number +44 (0) 1993 848726.

Bulk orders: some organisations buy a number of copies of our books. If you are interested in doing this, we would be pleased to discuss a discount. Please contact on email info@chandospublishing.com or telephone +44 (0) 1223 891358.

New Approaches to E-Reserve

Linking, sharing and streaming

OPHELIA CHEUNG, DANA THOMAS AND
SUSAN PATRICK

Chandos Publishing

Oxford • Cambridge • New Delhi

Chandos Publishing
TBAC Business Centre
Avenue 4
Station Lane
Witney
Oxford OX28 4BN
UK
Tel: +44 (0) 1993 848726
Email: info@chandospublishing.com
www.chandospublishing.com

Chandos Publishing is an imprint of Woodhead Publishing Limited

Woodhead Publishing Limited
Abington Hall
Granta Park
Great Abington
Cambridge CB21 6AH
UK
www.woodheadpublishing.com

First published in 2010

ISBN:
978 1 84334 509 1

British Library Cataloguing-in-Publication Data.
A catalogue record for this book is available from the British Library.

Typeset by RefineCatch Limited, Bungay, Suffolk
Printed in the UK and USA.

Printed in the UK by 4edge Limited - www.4edge.co.uk

Contents

List of figures

Introduction

How e-reserve responds to a changing user culture and copes with issues and challenges

E-reserve service in libraries has been in existence since the 1990s. It was started as an electronic counterpart of print reserve (or paper reserve), which has a much longer history, dating back to the nineteenth century. Both reserve services have the same objective: facilitating students' access to course-related materials assigned by faculty. Reserve materials include copies of journal articles, chapters from books or entire books, exams, tests, videos, CDs and lecture notes. In the case of print reserve, students visit the library and check out the physical materials for several hours or days. E-reserve, on the other hand, provides 24/7 online access to these materials. As long as there is access to a computer and the Internet, students can simply click on electronic links to documents or audio video files to view or hear the full content.

How libraries and universities respond to the changing user culture

E-reserve is constantly evolving and adapting to the changing technological and educational environment. These changes are in line with the challenges that confront libraries – a basic shift in user culture and learning behavior. Technology has undoubtedly played a large role in shaping a culture that values portability, connectivity and social interaction, not only in one's personal life or a recreational setting but also in the working and educational environment. Universities currently cater to three distinct generations of students, the 'Baby Boomers' born in the post-war era

1945–59, the sixties and seventies-born 'Generation-X', and new students of the 'Millennial' generation born in or after the year 1982 (Oblinger, 2003). Millennials have also been referred to as the Internet Generation, Echo Boomers, the Boomlet, Nexters, Generation Y, the Nintendo Generation and the Digital Generation (Raines, 2002). Almost all the Millennial generation of users possess cell phones, MP3s, iPods, digital cameras, notebooks, netbooks and other mobile devices. A mobile devices survey run in November 2008 at Ryerson University in Toronto, Ontario, Canada, found that only 3.2% of participants do not own a cell phone, 77.2% of those surveyed own regular cell phones, 20.7% already own smart phones, and an additional 64% intend to purchase a smart phone as their next phone. In addition, 32% would purchase a non-phone mobile device with WiFi Internet access such as an iPod Touch. The survey was completed by 811 people, 84% of whom were undergraduate students (Wilson, 2009). Their portable and digital gadgets have features that integrate listening, viewing, downloading and sharing of audio visual data and instant messaging that is voice-based, text-based, and picture-based. They are used to the convenience of wireless Internet access, searching aids such as GPS and audio visual displays such as Webcams and are accustomed to being able to connect with anyone or any place they wish, regardless of geographic location and time. Wikis and social bookmarking encourage the sharing of reading and writing experiences and sites like Facebook, Twitter, YouTube, and Flickr have pushed the envelope of social interaction and file sharing to the maximum. A person can share his or her photographs, videos and broadcast his or her own thoughts and ideas, and record and disseminate any daily life activities with any group that has a common interest. The Millennials have distinct learning behaviors such as preferring teamwork and experiential activities, use of technology for communication via email or instant messaging and socialization (Oblinger, 2003). They have the 'information-age mindset' including 'zero tolerance for delay', 'multitasking way of life' and 'staying connected' (Frand, 2000: 16–22). They are accustomed to 'multiprocessing' (Brown, 2000: 13) – listening to music, talking on the mobile phone and using the computer. Frand (2000) concurred that they are able to watch TV, talk on the phone, do homework, eat, and interact with their parents all at the same time. Indeed, this generation can do many of these things simultaneously. Their multitasking abilities are boundless.

In the face of these changes in user behavior, characteristics, preferences and expectations, how can libraries remain untouched by this new digital culture? How can libraries still expect students to access materials only available during certain hours and at a certain location? How will students react to a Web page loaded with library jargon, a language almost completely foreign to them, which requires them to search high and low before finding an answer to their question? Colleges and universities are changing their public image from a protective ivory tower to a more accessible, networked and communication-rich environment (Hanna, 2003). Libraries have also changed significantly in recent years in their design and delivery of services, from mainly collection-based to user-centered or user-driven environments. Print journals have given way to electronic and online subscriptions, including archival storage, providing the flexible access users desire. E-books are becoming more popular for the same reason. Videos-on-demand and streaming of multimedia on the Web are beginning to replace the VHS and DVD formats and physical viewing stations, increasing the ubiquity of access. Virtual reference has tremendously improved upon 24- and 48-hour email reference services in offering real-time interactive chat, often during hours the physical library is closed. Libraries are providing connectivity, demonstrating sensitivity to users' preferred search modes, and accommodating students' own preferences, allowing them to install widgets to a personalized iGoogle or NetVibes home page in the library catalogue. Google Books links can be added to the library's online public access catalogue (OPAC), enhancing the user experience by providing full text searching and previews. These links enable users to read passages of the book online before venturing into the library or placing a hold on unavailable materials. Libraries are investigating ways to provide resources and services to students' mobile devices, including cell phones, and iTunes U allows users to download audio or video course materials to their portable devices. Universities as a whole are responding to the changes in student culture and learning behavior, and academic institutions are offering a blended or hybrid learning environment, even to on-campus students. Virtual learning environments (VLE), course management systems (CMS), or learning management systems (LMS) are now commonplace, giving students the one-stop shopping experience of online learning, including interacting with instructors and peers, submitting assignments, receiving grades and maintaining their own e-portfolios.

Ryerson University Library has been proactive in responding to this Millennial digital culture. Ryerson is an urban university with a student body of approximately 25,000 undergraduate and graduate students. It is known for its innovative programs built on the integration of theoretical and practical learning, with more than 95 undergraduate and graduate programs, distinguished by a professionally focused curriculum. Ryerson is also a leader in adult education, with the largest university-based continuing education school in Canada.

In 2008, the Ryerson Library programmer initiated several projects to expand access to resources beyond the traditional confines of the building and the Website. These included integrating the library with Facebook, creating widgets for NetVibes and Google home pages, integrating library catalogue holdings with Amazon, Google Books and Indigo/Chapters Bookstore, and enabling text messaging from the library catalogue (McCarthy, Banerjee & Wilson, 2008). Once users have configured their Firefox browser using the library's instructions, they can easily see whether the Ryerson Library owns books, and view their current status from Amazon, Google Books, and Indigo/Chapters. The text messaging feature allows patrons to send title, call number, and location information to their cell phones and then view it later on their phone when they arrive in the book stacks (Wilson, 2009). In September 2009, Ryerson Mobile Applications (R mobile) went live. These applications are being developed by a multi-disciplinary team of student, staff and faculty representatives from the Library, Computing and Communications Services, Department of Computer Science (Ryerson Ubiquitous and Pervasive Computing Lab) and Students in Free Enterprise (SIFE). The following R mobile phone apps have been developed in response to student need: campus maps, campus directory, news and events, student schedules, booking library study rooms, finding available computers on campus, and accessing the library catalogue. Because of these mobile and texting enhancements to the libraries' digital environment, it is now common for students to come to the reference desk, show staff their phone display and say, 'I want this book.'

As librarians from Ryerson University, the authors of this work have intimate knowledge of these developments that respond to the changing needs of students. Ryerson Library's experiences will be discussed throughout the book, in addition to extensive literature reviews, library visits, surveys and communication with colleagues at conferences and other venues. Also included are examples from other parts of the world, such as Australia and Hong Kong, to provide a context beyond North America.

Overview of e-reserve

Chapter 2 provides an overview of the various approaches to electronic reserve that support the changing user culture. Traditional e-reserve was a standalone system, maintained by library staff. Hard copies of documents provided by faculty were converted by staff to digital formats, and then added to the OPAC of an integrated library system (ILS) such as Innovative Interfaces. The ILS may also contain a sub-module for handling e-reserve materials. Alternatively, some institutions have developed home-grown, dedicated systems or purchased a commercially produced system specifically designed for e-reserve support (such as Docutek's ERes). A newer route of delivery is via the Virtual Learning Environment (VLE), the Course Management System (CMS) or Learning Management System (LMS), which are often the academic institution's portal. Notable examples of these systems include WebCT, Blackboard and Angel. Open-source software that permits others to use, change, modify and redistribute content has emerged as an alternative to proprietary CMS, LMS, or commercial e-reserve systems. Free, community source and educational software that can be utilized as course management systems include Sakai and Moodle. ReservesDirect, also open-source software, was designed by Emory University in the United States, specifically to support e-reserve operations. Others have implemented creative alternatives to e-reserve systems and free products and software purchased for other purposes have been adapted to meet the library's needs while avoiding additional system costs. Examples include integrating the university's digital repository with their CMS/LMS, utilizing citation management software such as RefWorks, or employing iTunes U to deliver audio and video files.

Traditional and creative approaches to e-reserve

Chapter 3 explains in detail, using Blackboard as an example, how libraries can achieve integration of e-reserve with CMS/LMS in various ways. CMSs or LMSs are often administered by the academic institutions' Information Technology (IT) staff. The course shells (the area in the CMS/LMS where faculty create documents and set permissions for access) are controlled by faculty, who may not want access by a third party like library staff. Some libraries are therefore not able to make full use of the e-reserve module within a CMS/LMS like Blackboard, for linking and loading records. Instead, workarounds are created such as a building block between Blackboard and a library-created database of e-reserve content or importing cartridges of pre-created readings into Blackboard course pages.

Chapter 4 describes creative approaches to e-reserve, utilizing or adapting software not specifically designed for creating online readings. An institution's learning or digital objects repository includes the digital output of faculty and students created in the course of learning, teaching, research, and class assignments. The objects include lecture notes, theses, dissertations and multimedia projects. Library resources such as scanned book chapters, online journal articles, audio, video and image files may also be part of the digital content and selected as course materials to be integrated with the VLE, CMS or LMS.

The emergence of Web-based citation software provides another opportunity for innovation in e-reserve. RefWorks is a Web-based citation manager that allows users to collect, save and organize bibliographic citations to journal articles, books, Websites and other sources that were found during research. With it users can create correctly formatted bibliographies in the style of their choice. RefWorks is described as an example of using citation management software to create links to course readings, as well as providing the added value of correct citations and facilitating communication between instructor and students on a specific reading.

iTunes software was originally designed as a distribution channel for purchasing and downloading music to an iPod. New generations of iPods include color display for content such as music videos, movies and television programs that users can purchase or rent through iTunes. A further development for educational purposes is iTunes U, allowing colleges and universities to reach a wide audience for marketing, recruitment or public relations purposes. Some institutions like Stanford University in the United States and the United Kingdom's Open University have made use of the free iTunes U platform to deliver educational materials, such as lectures, interviews, promotional videos, podcasts and video tutorials to the public. While the authors could not identify an institution using iTunes U specifically for e-reserve purposes, there are examples of integration between iTunes U and CMS/LMS. Potentially, iTunes U could be utilized as a platform for instructional audio and video content integrated with a course.

Chapter 5 focuses on another format of e-reserve – video streaming. The case study of the development of a streaming project at Ryerson University Library illustrates the difficult issues involved. There were technical issues such as bandwidth, media platforms and also copyright constraints. There were choices to be made, as streaming options include in-house digitization, acquiring digital rights for individual streamed videos to be shown to restricted groups, or negotiating a campus-wide subscription to media databases.

How e-reserve responds to changes and issues encountered

The delivery of electronic reading lists on a chosen platform is one thing. The management, processing and maintenance of these readings can be a very different matter. Most course management systems do not have a sophisticated e-reserve module that addresses the complexities of the e-reserve process and copyright is a major concern. Most users, faculty and students alike, expect everything they need or want to be available in its entirety – free, downloadable, and accessible anywhere, anytime. However, under the current copyright legislation in many countries, libraries are not always able to reconcile users' needs or expectations with copyright constraints. Staff and patrons have to grapple with the ambiguity of fair use or fair dealing applications in the digital education environment in order to comply with the law. Keeping track of document access for royalty payment purposes or seeking copyright permissions for documents deemed to be not fair to the interests of the creators or authors are still common tasks that require the support of a well-structured database.

What constitutes links to electronic documents or other non-text materials such as videos? Apart from outlining the various e-reserve systems or software, Chapter 6 explains fully what URL stands for, why links break, and how to create a stable URL or permanent link and embed it in a course document. Scanning print material is one way of creating an e-reserve document. Links to electronic materials can be created in a variety of ways, such as copying and pasting the URL of a Web document or making use of an OpenURL link resolver, like SFX, to present all links to currently available article databases. The advantage of the SFX approach is that students will encounter a consistent path to library materials, whether from the library catalogue, journal article menu and databases, Wikipedia, Google Scholar or the institution's course management system. E-reserve documents are not limited to single chapters of books or articles, as links can be made to e-books, playlists created in a multimedia database or streamed video. Indeed, e-reserve's role has expanded to integrate with the wide array of digital resources and services offered by the library and the many different facets of online learning provided by the parent institution.

User perception, expectations and satisfaction present the next big challenge to e-reserve operations. How can libraries make users understand that not everything is free, when they seem to be able to obtain information free from the Internet? How can library staff explain why users cannot find the required readings as easily as they Google Internet resources, why whole books cannot be scanned and printed as they wish? Library database metadata and search strategy design, copyright, digital licenses, technical infrastructure, and other barriers all play a part in this apparent failure to measure up to users' expectations, and in their lack of understanding of e-reserve. For staff and e-reserve operations, the impact of cost, copyright restrictions and subsequent record keeping is the most tangible issue. For users, access to e-reserve content via a different system, especially if password protected, creates an extra authentication step and inconvenience. E-reserve is faced with more competition than traditional print or paper reserve (which only has to compete with course packs created by universities' bookstores for sale to students). In the case of online course readings, faculty have a variety of alternatives to choose from to allow access. They may not want to learn a new LMS or CMS or any system at all, and simply deliver information via their own Web page. There are commercially produced packages currently on the market, claiming to provide comprehensive content for customized selection. Some of them provide added value to the learning process by offering features such as quizzes, film strips, grading, and discussion boards, thus taking on the role of a learning management system as well as being a content provider. Another example of competition with e-reserve arose with the emergence of podcasting, providing an accessible option for audio visual content such as lectures and seminars and other presentations. Through user friendly publishing tools, faculty do not have to go through the library to post their learning materials on the Web. Chapter 6 discusses some of these complications faced by e-reserve operations.

Strategies to deal with challenges

Whatever challenges are ahead for e-reserve, *integration*, *collaboration* and *interaction* are keystones for survival and service expansion. Challenges often provide the opportunities for creative exploitation of existing resources, and formation of new alliances with other library services and stakeholders within the institution. Partnerships can flourish among groups sharing the common objective of enhancing the teaching and learning process in the new digital world, and the new approaches to e-reserve are indicative of strategies necessary to cope with the challenges brought about by change. To embrace these as opportunities and to make the most of them is to succeed; to dodge and avoid them is to eventually be swept away. In the final chapter (Chapter 7), the authors offer insights and learning experiences, and provide examples from other academic institutions on ways of addressing these issues. The case study of Ryerson University Library's E-Reserve operation is a microcosm of the strategies for dealing with change. Within a few months of its inception, the service was quick to seize the opportunity to grow, moving from delivering electronic readings solely via the OPAC, to collaborating with the university's IT department to embed e-reserve within Blackboard (Ryerson's course management system) as well. The Ryerson Library's willingness to take risks and its openness to collaboration was further illustrated by the adoption of the SFX link resolver to generate e-reserve article links, the experiment with RefWorks' RefShare to encourage faculty to create their own links, and the administrative support provided by the library to Distance Education for obtaining digital rights for video streaming. While Ryerson's E-Reserve unit may not be in a position to alter the copyright climate independently, the positive attitude shown by taking on the promotion of copyright literacy within the university was a step towards this goal.

Systems limitations can create another group of challenges. As Ryerson's E-Reserve service became more popular with faculty and students, staff increasingly felt the constraints of utilizing the e-reserve sub-module within Blackboard. Course management systems cannot provide the support desired for large-scale processing of faculty requests and copyright files management, and creating a separate database on MS Access and Excel was not efficient either. Ryerson Library had to start thinking about how to integrate a dedicated e-reserve system with content delivery within Blackboard.

E-reserve display can have an impact on user satisfaction as the organization of content and linking levels can influence ease of use. On the users' side, there was sufficient feedback from students to warrant a review of the practice of using the SFX menu of article access options versus a direct link to the document full text.

External competition is constant. Within and without the institution, other educational stakeholders are exploring ways to support the new digital culture and user learning behavior. Some examples include publishers' digital course pack initiatives and advances in online audio visual access. Faculty are increasingly drawn to the open access movement to avoid the copyright permission process, so e-reserve will have to continually evaluate its usefulness and effectiveness in satisfying users' needs and be prepared for radical changes, administrative or technological, when necessary.

2

Overview of e-reserve

History and scope

The concept of library reserve, a physical collection of high-use and short-term loan materials for quicker circulation, emerged as far back as in the nineteenth century. Electronic reserve or e-reserve was started in the United States in the early 1990s, as a 'collection of digital course materials made available over one or more computer networks' (Kristof, 1999: 1), and San Diego State University was the first library in 1993 to report an experiment with delivering course reading materials through such a network. While 1991–4 was the experimentation phase, when only a few libraries piloted the electronic approach to managing their high-use collections, 1995–9 witnessed the fastest development, resulting in a proliferation of electronic reserves (Austin, 2002). A literature review indicated that an estimated 250 e-reserve systems were in production in the United States in 1999 (Lu, 2001). Similar to the United States, e-reserves emerged in Australian academic libraries in the mid 1990s. According to a CAUL (Council of Australian University Librarians) information sharing exchange conducted by the University of Western Australia Library in January 2003 (Poleykett & Benn, 2003), at least 25 Australian academic libraries were operating, piloting, or developing some form of online reserve. Most of the libraries surveyed provided access to their electronic reading lists via the Integrated Library System (ILS).

Though the authors could not locate an extensive survey to confirm that most libraries use the ILS, this is probably still the case with a lot of e-reserve operations today. Seneca College in Toronto, Ontario, Canada conducted an informal survey in 2005 of e-reserve projects in the country (Peters-Lise et al., 2006). Based on the responses of 17 e-reserve projects across the country, ten commonalities were identified. Top of the list was the use of an ILS. Eight projects (47%) provided access through the library's OPAC; very few offered additional access through a course management system such as Blackboard or WebCT. Four libraries (24%) used an in-house system, two libraries (12%) used Websites while another two libraries (12%) used Docutek's ERes, a commercial dedicated system.

Ryerson University librarians conducted an online survey of e-reserve operations in December 2008 (see Appendix I). The questionnaire was posted on an e-reserve listserv and Ryerson librarians also e-mailed the survey link to several universities in Australia. Out of a total of 57 responses, 30 institutions (52%) used one system only for e-reserve and commercial software was the top choice (11 institutions or 19%), followed by ILS/OPAC (10 institutions or 17%) and course management software (6 institutions or 10%).

One of the authors visited five libraries in Hong Kong, China in 2008. There were eight universities in the city and at that time, three offered access directly via their library catalogues, accessible by course name or instructor name. One university library provided access to e-reserve materials from the Library Content module of their Blackboard course management system but the links were external, bringing students back to the library catalogue's alphabetical list of reading materials by document titles.

The ILS approach

The ILS approach does have its attractions. First, it is low cost, and low maintenance, as the library does not have to budget for or train staff in the use of another system. Secondly, the cataloguing templates are similar, so reports and statistics can be generated in a similar way. Thirdly, print and e-reserve materials are grouped in one location, accessible by course name and instructor name. Students do not have to grapple with another system interface. Figure 2.1 is a screenshot of Ryerson University Library's catalogue on the Innovative Interfaces' Millennium system.

There are shortcomings with this approach, however. The list displayed is usually limited to an alphabetical title/author list, with minimal bibliographic data (see Figure 2.2).

When problems occur, students do not know the source of the document (e.g. an article from a particular database) and staff cannot help to diagnose the problem easily. Faculty cannot organize materials in the way they like – by week, by topic or integrated with their own course page. The interactive element is lacking, as faculty cannot annotate individual records, nor can they communicate with students on these assigned readings. The collaborative element is non-existent, as there is no support for group work on a particular item within the reading list.

Figure 2.1 Search library catalogue for course readings

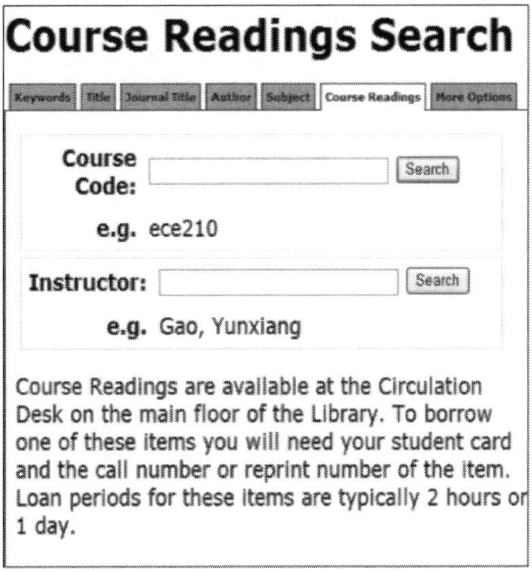

Course Readings Search

Keywords | Title | Journal Title | Author | Subject | **Course Readings** | More Options

Course Code: [ ] Search

e.g. ece210

Instructor: [ ] Search

e.g. Gao, Yunxiang

Course Readings are available at the Circulation Desk on the main floor of the Library. To borrow one of these items you will need your student card and the call number or reprint number of the item. Loan periods for these items are typically 2 hours or 1 day.

From Ryerson University Library, Toronto, Ontario, Canada.
Innovative Interfaces Millennium system by Innovative Interfaces. Used by permission.

Figure 2.2 Limited display format in library catalogue

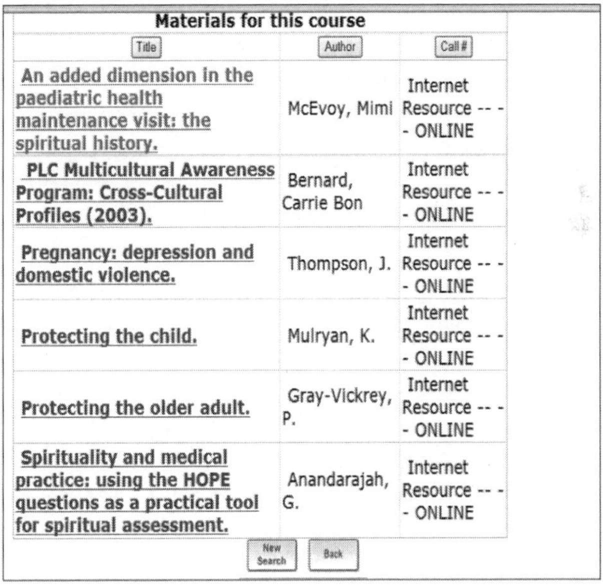

Materials for this course		
Title	Author	Call #
An added dimension in the paediatric health maintenance visit: the spiritual history.	McEvoy, Mimi	Internet Resource -- - - ONLINE
PLC Multicultural Awareness Program: Cross-Cultural Profiles (2003).	Bernard, Carrie Bon	Internet Resource -- - - ONLINE
Pregnancy: depression and domestic violence.	Thompson, J.	Internet Resource -- - - ONLINE
Protecting the child.	Mulryan, K.	Internet Resource -- - - ONLINE
Protecting the older adult.	Gray-Vickrey, P.	Internet Resource -- - - ONLINE
Spirituality and medical practice: using the HOPE questions as a practical tool for spiritual assessment.	Anandarajah, G.	Internet Resource -- - - ONLINE

New Search | Back

From Ryerson University Library, Toronto, Ontario, Canada.
Innovative Interfaces Millennium system by Innovative Interfaces. Used by permission.

13

Another big issue is the lack of security control. Copyright owners and publishers often require access to be restricted not just on an institution basis but at a course or class-specific level. Issuing group or class passwords is a solution but is labor intensive for library staff, cumbersome for instructors, and inconvenient for students who are used to the *click and get it* mode. From the staff perspective, since the ILS does not have a copyright tracking or management mechanism, everything has to be recorded separately on a spreadsheet or in a separate database, with practically no interface with the ILS. Realizing the limitations of an ILS, especially in dealing with copyright, some libraries have developed their own system or purchased a system dedicated to e-reserve operations.

The dedicated e-reserve system approach

Proprietary systems

A dedicated system satisfies most of the e-reserve requirements. The system can keep track of copyright access and payment, generate statistics, allow library staff to retain control, and offer users password-protected access to documents stored on the system. ERes was created by Docutek, a U.S. company founded in 1995. Docutek was acquired in January, 2005 by SirsiDynix Corporation, a company that develops and sells integrated library systems in the United States. In 2008, SirsiDynix Docutek announced the latest version of CCC Connect. This enhancement enabled direct integration with CCC's (Copyright Clearance Center in the United States) rights licensing database to obtain copyright permissions within the ERes workflow, and to update document visibility automatically. The new 5.5.1 release (found at *http://www.docutek.com/products/eres/ modules.html#mod_black*) promised convenience in handling copyright for instructors and staff. When an instructor creates a materials request, he or she can make use of a copyright fees calculator to estimate the cost in advance. The library can accept or deny the request, based upon this information. Requests can be sorted by any criteria and viewed at different stages of the processing workflow, while the instructor can use the Reserve Workflow list to check the status of request. When the request is approved, the library creates the document as part of the workflow, and the instructor links it with the proper course. Forms creation has been made easier as library staff can drag and drop fields from a list to create a form, determine their order and field names and customize existing forms for local need.

The ERes DocuFax feature, which was also available in earlier versions, enables instructors to fax their documents to e-reserve staff. These documents are automatically converted to PDF files, thus saving much time and labor in scanning. While primarily an electronic reserve system, ERes has expanded to include communication tools such as a virtual reference system that allows students, instructors and librarians to communicate with one another.

Ares (found at *http://www.atlas-sys.com/products/ares*) is another e-reserve system that manages the copyright process. Developed by Atlas, a company that sells integrated library systems, the Ares software was officially launched in 2005 in the United States. Integration of CCC's copyright permissions capabilities within Ares was added in 2006, making it possible to automatically cross-check permission requests that are stored in Ares with titles covered under CCC's License. Searching and modifying permissions for copyrighted materials can be done within Ares. Besides having a direct link to CCC, the system includes the ability to track copyright obtained and paid for outside of the CCC gateway, and the flexibility to match local sites' interpretation of copyright guidelines. Similar to Docutek ERes, the Ares system was also designed to improve e-reserve staff workflow and user interface. The system caters to different faculty needs – uploading documents themselves, sending bibliographic information to library staff to create e-reserve documents on their behalf, filling out a Web-based request form that can be populated via an OpenURL request from a compatible database or using a text editor to create documents on the fly. Students, too, can create a hot list of items, subscribe to e-mail updates or RSS feeds when faculty add new reserve items to their class. In addition to faculty functionalities, the staff interface integrates into the software: Z39.50 client-server protocol catalogue searching, retrieval slip printing capability, and a scanning feature. System alerts can be dispatched, such as announcements about library hours and policy changes. As well as using the standard statistical reports generated by the Ares software, local sites can manage their own reports using software such as MS Access or Excel. Libraries can design their own procedures to create a customized Web interface, using the Customization Manager, and standard HTML in the template. These special features are rarely found within an integrated library system or a learning management system (Calsada, 2006).

Although it is useful to have a system designed specifically for e-reserve operations, acquiring an additional system comes with extra cost, maintenance and a learning curve, however user-friendly the system may be. The capability to customize also varies with local circumstances.

Bucknell University in Pennsylvania, United States, for example, has noted inadequacies in Docutek's ERes to customize some pages or locate certain usage statistics (Hiller, 2004). Multiple steps were needed to add a document to a page. Difficulties were encountered in cross listing courses, deleting faculty accounts and creating non-course pages for guest speakers and committee reports. Faculty found it inconvenient to assign and distribute passwords for each individual course. ERes' new releases might address some of these shortcomings, but as the example above illustrates, no matter how good the design of the system for generic use, gaps will still exist between local demands and what the system offers. The copyright management features of Docutek's ERes or Atlas' Ares were designed for applications in the United States, so some of these features may not be applicable to institutions in other countries. The direct link to CCC is not relevant for institutions that do not make use of its service. Owing to differences in copyright legislation, these institutions cannot fully utilize the copyright component in the software or the fax to PDF feature. They may still need to maintain copyright analysis work and permission requests on another platform. In hard economic times, libraries will consider very seriously the cost of acquiring and maintaining a dedicated system, in addition to their own integrated library system. For example, Drake Memorial Library, State University of New York in the United States, had been using Docutek ERes since 1998 but decided to change to the Angel learning management system in 2004 (O'Hara, 2006). There were many reasons for such a major change, including concerns with staff workload for electronic reserve and overlap between Angel and ERes software in key areas (e.g. posting documents, adding links, chat rooms, and bulletin boards). Library staff used to be involved in creating course pages, adding instructors and creating passwords. However, since Angel was pre-populated with this information and authentication could be done through the proxy server, library staff no longer had to input this data in ERes. Above all, O'Hara (2006: 38) noted that 'as with many projects, the compelling reason for change was cost: a software savings of $5,000 per year', as well as savings in technical support for the ERes server, managing software upgrades and fixing bugs.

Home-grown systems

The development of an in-house system is meant to address local needs. A study from the Association of Research Libraries (ARL) in the United States

(Kristof, 1999) found that more than half (59%) of the respondents offering e-reserve had home-grown systems. A few variations of these systems were summarized, including the use of an html Website and OPAC to point to reserve documents on a Web server, integrating reserve services with a campus course management system or creating a 'database driven Web application' (Wynstra, 2005: 62). While the advantage of these undertakings is customization to local needs, the complexities and time required must be factored into the equation.

The University of Calgary's Allectra is a good example of the amount of technical support required for a home-grown system (Pearce, 2001). Allectra is a fully featured electronic reserve platform developed by the University of Calgary in Alberta, Canada in the early 2000s. A librarian involved in the development described it as 'a major undertaking, requiring literally years of dedicated labour'. There were constant changes in software specifications, a need for new standards, and acquisition and configuration of hardware. The reliance on programming support was enormous. At one stage, a complete rewrite using Java server pages, and MySQL as the underlying Database Management System (DBMS) was planned, in order to add functionality with XML. The project direction was eventually changed due to programming staff turn-over. As Kesten (2002) pointed out, the cost of developing an e-reserve system is often under-estimated:

> By far, the single most significant factor in the cost to develop a homegrown system is the salary of staff, students or consultants who design and create the software. This is often a hidden or 'sunk' cost, however, and in most cases, no budget process is required. As a result, the price tag to develop a homegrown system may appear to be much lower than the real cost to the Library. (Rosedale, 2002: 159)

Open source systems

Most institutions, especially smaller ones, cannot afford the robust in-house technical and programming support required to design and implement their own e-reserve system. As an alternative, institutions turn to open source software to achieve customization. The benefits of open source projects are that other sites can extend the program, and participating institutions share the outcome of modification or re-design. There were several open source course reserve projects in the United States, such as Open Source Course Reserve (OSCR), found at *http://iso.gmu.edu?OSCR*, and ReservesDirect, found at *http://www.reservesdirect.org/*. OSCR was developed initially at George Mason University and Grotophorst and Frumkin (2002) described in detail the project 'OSCR: Open Source Software and Electronic Reserves' in a book on electronic reserves, edited by Jeff Rosedale. This open source initiative suggested some possible future directions, including XML import features and an API (Application Programming Interface) to integrate with campus systems.

While the advantage of this approach is the free software available, participating institutions cannot discount altogether the amount of technical expertise required to first install the software, to configure it for the local environment, and then to invest in the ongoing maintenance of its operations. The development of Emory University's ReservesDirect, found at *http://www.reservesdirect.org/wiki/index.php/Documentation:_ About_ReservesDirect* illustrates some key issues in designing an open-source system. Users' demands are never static and the system has to be flexible and scalable for their changing needs. System support is not a one-time investment but an on-going one. At its worst, the whole system may have to be overhauled to accommodate new demands that were not anticipated in the original design. The Emory University system was designed initially in 2001 to address a need to sort and annotate reading lists, a requirement not met by their ILS-based reserves package. Increased popularity of e-reserve and the impact on staff workload at the beginning of each semester prompted the development of a more flexible system that would enable faculty to manipulate their own lists. A system was developed later that allowed instructors to upload documents, fax in articles that were converted to PDF, create multiple levels of permission to edit a class, and export reserve lists to Blackboard, using RSS link that updated Blackboard when changes were made in ReservesDirect. The system went live in 2003 and was released as an open source project on SourceForge, found at *http://sourceforge.net/ projects/coursecontrol/*. However, soon after its 2003 release, inadequacies were discovered, as faculty requested more functionality to accommodate multiple manipulation of the same list for team teaching. This was not anticipated in the initial design. The development team concurred that to meet such needs, revising the existing system was impossible. The whole system was then completely rewritten based on MySQL and PHP5. ReservesDirect2 went live in 2004, but the developments were not final. A major release was expected each summer and regular updates were planned throughout the year. Without on-going systems support and staff time, open-source systems are hard to maintain.

The CMS, LMS or VLE approach

Despite the commonality of offering digitized readings via the library catalogue or ILS, there has been a tendency in recent years for e-reserve operations to move towards students' virtual learning environment (VLE), the Learning Management System (LMS) or Course Management System (CMS). CMS or LMS are technology that provides support for flexible learning. Collis and De Boer gave a very detailed description of the system components. The Web-based course-management system was defined as 'a comprehensive software package that supports some or all aspects of course preparation, delivery, communication, participation and interaction and allows these aspects to be accessible via a network'. The many variations of the term were mentioned: 'some of these metaphoric, such as course in a box or virtual university; some more informative, such as electronic learning environments, virtual learning environments, course-support systems, or online educational delivery applications' (Collis & De Boer, 2004: 7). Such a system usually includes both student tools as well as teacher tools:

> Student tools can relate to web browsing, sharing and archiving of resources and work products, synchronous and asynchronous communication and collaboration, self-assessment and personal environments such as biography pages and digital portfolios. Teacher tools can include tools for course planning, managing and customizing; for lesson design and presentation; for managing assignments, feedback and (online) marking, as well as maintaining overall marks and records of student performance; and for creation, management and reuse of resources. All of these tools are generally made available via a uniform web-based user interface. The 'back-office' aspects of the system most commonly involve a combination of a database, database technology and an HTTP server (the type of computer software that allows a computer to perform as a web server). (Collis & De Boer, 2004: 7–8)

The emergence of Web-based learning has blurred the distinction between on-campus and off-campus learning. The technology that is used for distance learners can just as well be applied on campus to improve the quality of teaching and learning. Students want 24/7 access, anytime, anywhere. The Web has pervaded every facet of the teaching and learning processes: research and preparation of teaching or learning materials, one-on-one instruction via email or chat or ISM, shared interactive discourse through online discussion boards and grading of students' assignments. As more and more universities recognize the benefits of Web-based learning, even for on-campus students, and adopt some form of blended learning across the curriculum, the use of a CMS or LMS as the university's teaching and learning portal has become a global phenomenon. In a report, *Libraries and the enhancement of e-learning*, the E-Learning Task Force of Online Computer Library Center, Inc. (OCLC, 2003) described the astounding growth in the use of LMS or CMS between the years 2000 and 2002 in the United States. At Carnegie Mellon University, for example, the number of classes using Blackboard increased from 150 courses in 2000 to 567 in 2002 (Gerlich & Perrier, 2003).

Integrating e-reserves in the CMS or LMS has gained momentum in recent years. Poe and Skaggs (2007) referred to a 2004 study, conducted at Cornell University in the United States, to explore faculty perceptions of integrating electronically accessible library resources with the university's CMS or LMS. Faculty were asked to identify their top choices for library information to be integrated into the courseware. E-reserve was first on the list (42% or 35 responses), followed by subject databases (30% or 24 responses) (Rieger, Horne, & Revels, 2004). Warren (2005) compared the application of OpenURL with DOI (Digital Object Identifier) in e-reserve from the student perspective. Developed by the International DOI Foundation, a DOI name, found at *http://www.doi.org/faq.html#1*, is a digital identifier for any object of intellectual property. In his opinion, too much attention has been paid to the discovery process, the reference transactions and education of end users to search for documents, often in disregard of students' equally important demand for convenient access to reserve readings (pp. 2–3). Similarly, at Northwestern University in the United States, 'the most compelling argument to use Blackboard ... for e-reserves resides in its familiarity to faculty and students' (Cubbage, 2003: 25). Continuing with this student-centered focus, the OCLC (2003) report suggested that a courseware environment or VLE potentially could bring all resources, library owned or not owned, into one single Web space accessible by students.

Examples of CMS/LMS

There are various proprietary CMS and LMS on the market, the most notable being WebCT, Blackboard and Angel. WebCT, found at *http://*

www.webct.com/, was originally developed in 1994 at the University of British Columbia in Canada by a faculty member in computer science. His research showed that the use of Web-based course tools (from which the name WebCT is derived) was helpful in improving students' academic performance and satisfaction with learning. The WebCT product was launched commercially in 1997. In February 2006, WebCT was acquired by rival Blackboard Inc., found at *http://www.blackboard.com/*, a company founded in 1997 in Washington D.C. in the United States. The Angel LMS (Learning Management Suite), found at *http://www. angellearning.com/*, evolved from research at Indiana University-Purdue University in Indianapolis. Though marketed as a commercial application, Angel published their database schema and documents and their API to allow extension and integration with other systems or products. In May 2009, Angel was also acquired by Blackboard.

Sakai and Moodle are open-source software that permit others to use, change, modify, improve and redistribute. The Sakai CLE (Collaboration and Learning Environment), found at *http://sakaiproject.org/portal*, was released in 2005. It is a free, community source, educational software platform based mainly on the University of Michigan's course management system, and distributed under the Educational Community License. In addition to its course management features, Sakai allows changes in the tool settings based on user access, and includes a wiki, a mailing list, an archive and an RSS reader. Moodle, found at *http://moodle.org/*, was developed by Curtin University of Technology in Perth, Australia. Designed as a free, open-source software package, it can be downloaded and used on any computer. It can be implemented in any sized application, from a single-teacher site to a large university. Sakai is more common in the United States while Moodle is popular in Europe, Australia and Asia. One of the authors visited a university library in Hong Kong in 2007 and learnt that several faculty members pushed for the use of Moodle because other commercial systems were not able to handle the Chinese characters in the way they desired.

Pros and cons of e-reserve in LMS or CMS

There are advantages of using the LMS or CMS approach for e-reserve as faculty and students are familiar with the system and navigation pattern. Once logged into the LMS or CMS, the library's e-reserve materials are only a couple of clicks away and libraries do not have to spend extra money on a dedicated system to support e-reserve. There are ways to create sub-folders in the Blackboard Content System to arrange content in the desired way, such as by week or by topic. Although it is convenient to simply create an e-reserve folder and upload all readings into that folder, faculty can also copy and paste external links to documents within their course text so that the readings become an integral part of the course description or course notes.

Nevertheless, the Blackboard system is not without problems. Ryerson University Library has used Blackboard for e-reserve since 2004, but statistics gathering has been an issue. Extra programming is required before the raw data can provide a count of the number of times a PDF file is accessed by students. Some libraries in Hong Kong created links for faculty as an e-reserve service and emailed them to faculty for their own management in the CMS or LMS. Because library staff did not have any administrative access to course pages created by faculty, they did not know how the links were displayed. The different uses of Blackboard for e-reserve, and Ryerson Library's experience in using the eReserves module of Blackboard, are described in Chapter 3.

The repository-based approach

The development of e-reserve has taken an interesting turn by adapting to yet another new Web-based product – the Institutional Repository (IR). The term was first coined in 2001 by SPARC (the Scholarly Publishing & Academic Resources Coalition, Washington D.C). In the publication, *The case for institutional repositories: A SPARC position paper*, Crow (2002: 4) defined IR as 'digital collections capturing and preserving the intellectual output of a single or multi-university community', and also as 'a digital archive of the intellectual product created by the faculty, research staff, and students of an institution and accessible to end-users both within and outside of the institution, with few if any barriers to access' (Crow, 2002: 16).

Digital repositories can also be discipline based, developed and maintained by a subject community. For example, arXiv.org (Cornell University), found at *http://arxiv.org/*, provides open access to thousands of e-prints in Physics, Mathematics, Computer Science, Quantitative Biology, Quantitative Finance and Statistics. A paper on *The business of digital repositories* offered a comprehensive listing of functions or foci of digital repositories:

- To *open up and offer* the outputs of the institution or community to the world.

- To *impact on and influence* developments by maximizing the visibility of outputs and providing the greatest possible chance of enhanced impact as a result.

- To *showcase and sell* the institution to interested constituencies – prospective staff, prospective students and other stakeholders.

- To *collect and curate* digital outputs (or inputs, in the case of special collections).

- To *manage and* measure research and teaching activities.

- To provide and promote a workspace for work-in-progress, and for collaborative or large-scale projects.

- To facilitate and further the development and sharing of digital teaching materials and aids.

- To *support and sustain* student endeavours, including providing access to theses and dissertations and providing a location for the development of eportfolios. (Swan, 2008: 2)

IRs are now well established globally. In 2003, CNI (Coalition for Networked Information) surveyed over 200 individual higher education institutions in the United States (Lynch & Lippincott, 2005). About 40% of the respondents had some type of institutional repository operating, and 88% were planning to develop one or participate in some form. CARL (the Canadian Association of Research Libraries), found at *http:// www.carl-abrc.ca/about/about-e.html*, represents 29 university libraries in Canada plus Library and Archives Canada, the Canada Institute for Scientific and Technical Information (CISTI), and the Library of Parliament. CARL began an Institutional Repository Project in 2003 with the aim of assessing the IR concept in the Canadian context (Shearer, 2006). According to their 2005 survey of institution members, over 70 per cent have developed institutional repositories, embarked on pilot projects at their institutions or were planning to do so in the near future. There are many single and multi-institution IR projects in Europe. *ARNO* (Academic Research in the Netherlands Online), found at *https:// www.h-net.org/announce/show.cgi?ID=127076*, aims to 'develop and implement university document servers to make available the scientific output of participating institutions'. *DARE* (Digital Academic Repositories) found at *http://www.kb.nl/hrd/dd/dd_projecten/projecten_ dare-en.html* is a multi-university project by the Dutch universities to make all their research results digitally accessible. The *FAIR* programme, funded by the United Kingdom Joint Information Systems Committee, is another multi-university initiative. Fifty UK universities participated in the 14 major projects aimed 'to support access to and sharing of institutional content within Higher Education (HE) and Further Education (FE), and to allow intelligence to be gathered about the technical, organizational and cultural challenges of these processes' (Pinfield, 2003). SHERPA, found at *http://www.sherpa.ac.uk/about.html*, was originally formed by research-led universities in the United Kingdom for the SHERPA project (2002–6) in establishing an example of 'a then-new concept – an open access institutional repository'. The network now has a total of 33 partners and affiliates, consisting of 32 higher education institutions and the British Library.

How e-reserve is linked with digital repositories

Libraries realize that their parent institutions produce an ever-growing mass of data, images, multimedia works, learning objects and digital records. Other stakeholders in the Web world also create large-scaled digitized content collections. The location of the users or even the resources themselves is a lesser priority than a seamless entry into the digital content during the users' learning activities. In the same way that e-reserve entered into the arena of CMS or LMS, it has striven to be a part of the institution's repository of digital objects. A digital assets management system can be used to house digital collections (e.g. special collections), institutional repositories (e.g. electronic theses and dissertations) and learning and course materials used by faculty and students (e.g. exam papers and electronic readings). The University of Western Australia Library gave a detailed description of their migration process of e-reserve, as a decentralized electronic collection of high-used materials, into a centralized, institution-wide electronic repository of teaching and learning materials (Poleykett & Benn, 2003). Past examination papers, scanned journal articles and book chapters in PDF, and HTML documents representing links to online journal articles and Websites, were imported into the new repository from their old Learning Management System, and were then reassembled into reading lists.

Ohio State University in the United States had a pilot project, which they named *toolkit approach* (Black, 2008), to integrate library resources, including e-reserve materials, into the Desire2 Learn learning management system. Seneca College in Canada used ENCompass before 2008 (Peters-Lise, 2009). Their experience illustrated how e-reserve could be combined with a comprehensive digital collection management approach and a learning management system. In 2009 the college adopted DigiTool, developed by ExLibris, to manage its digital resources and created electronic reading materials accessible through Blackboard. More details on these projects will be discussed in Chapter 4, alongside the other creative approaches to e-reserve.

The citation management software approach

As subscriptions to citation management software became more commonplace in academic libraries, several institutions have begun using it for creative purposes. The software was originally designed as both a personal database for citations found during the course of research, and as a method of bibliography and reference list automation. Several libraries in Canada and the United States have utilized an existing subscription to citation management software to streamline the process of creating online reading lists. Some have also utilized this type of software to improve the organization and display of readings beyond what is available with existing tools and systems. Chapter 4 describes several examples of this approach, and offers methods libraries can use to mimic this approach using open source software.

The iTunes U approach

Launched for American institutions in 2007, Apple's iTunes U uses the popular music and video software for iPod to deliver educational content – both for public and institutionally-restricted consumption. The academic sites on iTunes U primarily utilize it as a distribution channel for public relations and promotional materials, podcasts (audio) and vodcasts (video) of class lectures and guest speakers, PDF reproductions of PowerPoint slides and course handouts. Based on a review of the literature, and a survey of publicly viewable iTunes U content, it is clear that libraries have seen the value of iTunes U primarily as a delivery method for library instructional videos, and promotional videos. To date, the authors have not seen an example of iTunes U for e-reserve. It is more likely that iTunes U is linked with CMSs like Blackboard to supplement reading lists there with audiovisual content in iTunes U. iTunes U, and its potential use for e-reserve, is discussed in greater detail in Chapter 4.

Linking methods

Regardless of the e-reserve approach utilized, some method of linking must be used to connect students with online readings which are under copyright restrictions. Methods including Digital Object Identifier (DOI) linking, persistent URL (PURL) linking, and OpenURL linking are described in Chapter 6.

3

Access and delivery of e-reserve (1)

Blackboard – how resources are integrated within a course management system

The Blackboard course management system is a popular CMS used by academic institutions in North America. Many institutions provide e-reserve via this platform. However, there is no single way of integrating e-reserve within Blackboard. The authors have identified five different approaches: adapting the Library Content feature within Blackboard; utilizing the system's eReserves module; creating a building block between library resources and the CMS; inserting Course Cartridges into the system; and finally, making use of the building block feature devised by commercial e-reserve software to achieve the integration.

Different methods of creating e-reserve content in Blackboard

Making use of Blackboard's Library Content area

The eReserves content area can be found in the Blackboard Content Management area. On the left menu, click on the Institution Content link to open a submenu for Library. There are two components: the Library Content and the eReserves (Figure 3.1).

The Library Content is an area where the library can post and share information and files, provided the permissions allow access to this folder. Permissions can be added to share the content of this folder with other staff in the department and can also be set at the file level to share the information with all campus accounts. One of the authors visited the City University of Hong Kong in 2006. At that time, Library Content was used

Figure 3.1   The Institution Content submenu

From Ryerson University Library, Toronto, Ontario, Canada.
Copyright © 2009 Blackboard Inc. Used by permission.

for sharing e-reserve content, but the university did not open up the e-reserve module within the Content System of Blackboard. Instead, e-reserve became part of the Library Content of Blackboard, collating with other library resources or services links such as subject guides and Ask A Librarian, under a browsable list of subjects or courses (Figure 3.2).

Figure 3.2   E-reserves in Library Content are external links to items in library catalogue

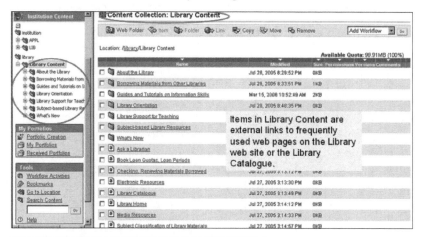

From Run Run Shaw Library, City University of Hong Kong.
Copyright © 2009 Blackboard Inc. Used by permission.

Blackboard eReserves module

The eReserves folder is the area where e-reserve materials and articles can be posted in Blackboard. Ryerson University Library is using this folder for storing e-reserve materials by course. The library obtains faculty permission to access their course shell and upload document links into course pages on their behalf. Ryerson Library also creates a dummy student account (Figure 3.3) so that Reference staff can access the e-reserve component of student course pages to understand what problems students have encountered and offer directions for help (Figure 3.4). (The sample pages were taken from Ryerson University's Professor Peter Kiatipis's Winter 2008 course – CRM306: Corrections in Canada.)

Figure 3.3 Library staff login as dummy student and see a list of courses that have course builder access

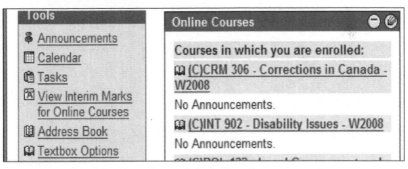

From Ryerson University Library, Toronto, Ontario, Canada.
Copyright © 2009 Blackboard Inc. Used by permission.

Figure 3.4 Library staff access e-reserve readings within a course page to answer students' queries

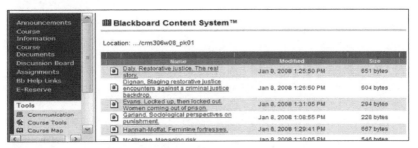

From course page of Peter Kiatipis, Assistant Professor, Department of Criminal Justice and Criminology. Ryerson University, Toronto, Ontario, Canada.
Copyright © 2009 Blackboard Inc. Used by permission.

The following instructions on creating folders and adding links within eReserves in Blackboard are based on the staff training materials prepared by the Digital Media Projects Office (DMP), Ryerson's Blackboard administrator.

Setting permissions

Only instructors have permissions to create and modify content in the course folders. However, permission can be obtained from instructors to add an E-Reserve account to the course as a Course Builder so that library staff can upload the links into faculty course pages (Figure 3.5).

Figure 3.5 User roles and course access within Blackboard

Access to Course Tools

	Instructor/ Leader	T.A./ Assistant	Course/Org Builder	Grader
Add Announcements	Yes	Yes	Yes	
Add/Modify Assignments	Yes	Yes	Yes	
Add/Modify Quizzes and Surveys	Yes	Yes	Yes	Yes
Add/Modify Deployment of Quizzes and Surveys	Yes	Yes	Yes	
Access/Modify Gradebook	Yes	Yes		Yes

From the Office of Digital Media Projects, Ryerson University, Toronto, Ontario, Canada. Copyright © 2009 Blackboard Inc. Used by permission.

Permissions to share with other courses

Once a course folder is created in eReserves, permissions are automatically set to allow all the course users (students, instructors) to view the content (Figure 3.6). If the instructor of this course wants this folder to be shared with other specific courses, permissions can be modified to allow users in the other courses to access the same folder (Figure 3.7).

Create and organize folders

All sorts of files, including Word documents, PowerPoint slides and PDF can be added to the course folder. To add a file, simply select the +Item (Add Item) on the top menu (Figure 3.8).

Add links to library reserve items

To add a link to the Library eReserves, click the +Link option. On the Add External Link page, enter the Link Name (name of the article), paste in the full URL and click Submit (Figure 3.9).

Figure 3.6 Setting permission to view eReserves content

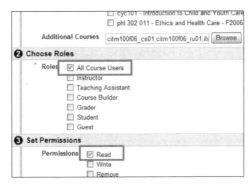

From the Office of Digital Media Projects, Ryerson University, Toronto, Ontario, Canada.
Copyright © 2009 Blackboard Inc. Used by permission.

Figure 3.7 Setting permissions to share content with other courses

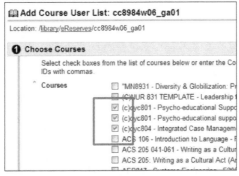

From the Office of Digital Media Projects, Ryerson University, Toronto, Ontario, Canada.
Copyright © 2009 Blackboard Inc. Used by permission.

Figure 3.8 Adding files to course folder

From the Office of Digital Media Projects, Ryerson University, Toronto, Ontario, Canada.
Copyright © 2009 Blackboard Inc. Used by permission.

Figure 3.9 Adding links to eReserves

From the Office of Digital Media Projects, Ryerson University, Toronto, Ontario, Canada. Copyright © 2009 Blackboard Inc. Used by permission.

E-reserve materials can be organized into sub-folders – by subject, by week or other groupings, at the discretion of the instructors. In the eReserves area select the course folder to work with. Look at the top options menu and select +Folder button (Figure 3.10). On the Add Folder page enter only the folder name and click Submit.

Figure 3.10 Adding folder

From the Office of Digital Media Projects, Ryerson University, Toronto, Ontario, Canada. Copyright © 2009 Blackboard Inc. Used by permission.

Building block between library resources and Blackboard

The method described above requires e-reserve staff to be given course builder permissions to enter instructors' course shells. Not every institution creates e-reserve content in Blackboard using this method, as faculty may want to retain control of their own course shells. Libraries have discovered alternatives to integrate e-reserve content into instructors' course shells in Blackboard, without the course builder permissions.

In September 2008, the University of Toronto in Canada introduced a way to embed library resources, including electronic readings, into their

Blackboard course delivery platform (Figures 3.11 and 3.12). A structural framework was built using RSS feeds that are auto-generated for each course and based on a pre-existing database of discipline-specific resources. The database consists of subject research guides and RefWorks/RefShare pages.

Figure 3.11   Sample library resources page in Blackboard

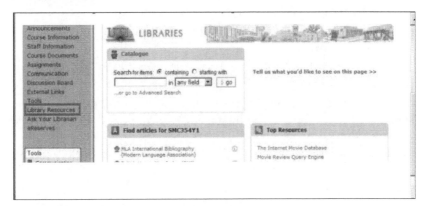

From University of Toronto Libraries, Ontario, Canada.
Copyright © 2009 Blackboard Inc. Used by permission.

Figure 3.12   Sample E-Reserves page in Blackboard

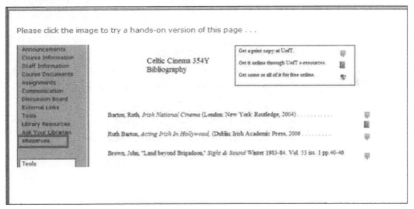

From University of Toronto Libraries, Ontario, Canada.
Copyright © 2009 Blackboard Inc. Used by permission.

In the event that the auto-populating process could not function, a fix-it tool has been developed to enable library staff to modify the RSS feeds and view the Web display in Blackboard, without seeking course access permission from individual instructors. The Web pages were 'repurposed for other course management system or standalone Web pages, making this a secure, flexible and scalable model' (Meikle & Vine, 2008). Of course, the creation of a building block requires programming support and the pre-existence of a library resources database that is discipline-specific and appropriately coded so that the matching with course pages can happen.

Inserting cartridges into Blackboard course shells

Another way of integrating e-reserve materials within Blackboard is utilizing the system's Course Cartridges feature. Course Cartridges were originally used by publishers to provide additional pre-packaged course materials for ready use in Blackboard. They contain a variety of materials including slides, documents, multimedia files, links to related Websites, test banks, and quizzes, and could be used along with a textbook, an eBook or for standalone purpose. Instructors would download these materials to their specific course sites.

Seneca College in Toronto, Canada had librarians customize the design of such a package of information. Instead of sending instructors individual links or documents, resources are added to a content area in Blackboard and exported into a cartridge, which are zipped files formatted by Blackboard. The advantage is that these cartridges can be used by more than one faculty member. The following sample instructions on how to import the APA Tutorial and Quiz Packages into a Seneca course (Figure 3.13) were provided by Jennifer Peters-Lise, Metadata & Digital Services Librarian (jennifer.peters-lise@senecac.on.ca).

According to Seneca College, creating links independently and outside of Blackboard has several advantages. As these links are created as part of their digital asset management system, their stability will not be affected. Archiving links for potential re-use will not impact on the speed of course delivery in Blackboard.

Integration of dedicated e-reserve systems with Blackboard

Developers of proprietary e-reserve systems have devised methods of integrating their software with course management systems. SirsiDynix ERes 5.5.1 release (found at *http://www.docutek.com/products/eres/modules.html#mod_black*) in December 2008 announced its new

Figure 3.13   Importing cartridges into course pages

Importing the Apa Tutorial and Quiz Package into a Myseneca Course

1. Save the *apa.zip* file to your desktop.

2. Sign-in to MySeneca. Open your course.

3. In the control panel of your course click on "Import Package".

4. Click on "browse" to find the *apa.zip* file on your desktop, then checkmark the 4 boxes highlighted below. Click "submit".

5. Click "okay" when you receive this message.

6. You may delete the email you will receive informing you that the action was successful.

7. After a couple of minutes the package will appear in your course's main menu, you may have to refresh your web page couple of times for the item to appear.

8. The results of the quiz will be automatically collected in Gradebook. You have the option to make them weighted and/c include them in your final calculations. For instructions please consult the MySeneca tip sheet.

Figure 3.13   Importing cartridges into course pages (Cont'd)

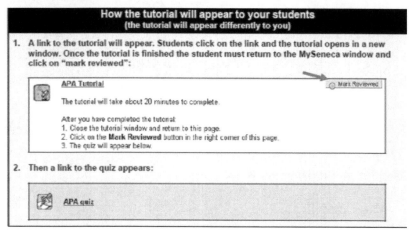

From Jennifer Peters-Lise, Metadata & Digital Services Librarian, Seneca College Libraries, Toronto, Canada.
Copyright © 2009 Blackboard Inc. Used by permission

function of integrating with Blackboard. Library staff can 'add content to ERes for automatic insertion in Blackboard' and can 'import courses and users into ERes from Blackboard'. Document lists can be updated within Blackboard and ERes can be connected directly to the Blackboard server, allowing end users to access ERes documents in Blackboard. In June 2009, ERes launched the streaming media option, allowing audio or video files to be streamed via the built-in streaming media player.

The Atlas Ares system has promoted one of its new features in Version 2.5 – Blackboard (E-Learning Platform Compatibility), found at *http://www.atlas-sys.com/products/ares/downloads/ares_2pg_web.pdf*. 'New courses can be created directly from Blackboard. Instructors, course builders and teaching assistants can create courses in Ares by clicking on the Course Reserves link under Class Tools or through the Control Panel.' The display options for Blackboard can be set to Class Link, taking the user to the Ares course page without another click on a separate link.

In January 2009, University of Guelph in Ontario, Canada announced a change in their e-reserve system interface from the library catalogue to Ares Course Reserves System that promises more customization to suit user needs. Instructors can view online past, present and future course lists, submit requests in any format, including PowerPoint and MP3 files, integrate with the course management system, and automatically notify students by e-mail or RSS feed when new reserve readings become available.

E-reserve in Blackboard: some insight and experiences

It is not uncommon for libraries to run parallel systems as e-reserve systems are operated concurrently with course management systems. Philadelphia University in the United States maintained their Docutek ERes system and Blackboard simultaneously (Bell & Krasulski, 2004). An argument was made for running e-reserve on both systems. Traditional e-reserve was a standalone system, maintained by library staff. Hard copies of documents provided by faculty were converted by staff to digital formats, and then added to the e-reserve system, either in a dedicated product such as Docutek ERes or an integrated library system such as Innovative Interfaces' Millennium or Endeavor's Voyager, with an e-reserve module. Given the multiplicity of systems and information databases available on campuses, it was decided that these systems be integrated to provide students with the most timely and convenient way to access course readings. E-reserve then became a complementary system to the campus-wide Blackboard course information system and increased the utility of the library online databases. Since every document added to their ERes course site has a unique URL, and Blackboard has a utility for creating external links to Websites, faculty just copied and pasted the URL into the Blackboard template. With the seamless connection between the two systems, students did not have to remember extra passwords or to learn different system interfaces. Library staff had the features of an e-reserve system, such as copyright management and DocuFax, which reduced or eliminated the scanning process.

Poe and McAbee (2008) described their six years' experience of integrating electronic reserve with the Blackboard system at Jacksonville State University in the United States. Library presence in the course management system demonstrates to the teaching faculty that the library is an 'essential part of the students' education and an effective collaborative partner. At the same time, it demonstrates to students that the library is the best place to start and finish their research – sometimes without ever leaving their computers' (p. 259).

Ryerson Library has chosen to open the e-reserve module within Blackboard's Content System to help faculty create e-reserve readings. During its five years of operation, the library has encountered many challenges. When Ryerson E-Reserve started its project in 2005, off-campus users had to use a separate login and password for Blackboard access to their courses and then a library barcode and PIN for remote access to links created from library subscribed databases. It is not hard to imagine the frustration experienced by students having to go through multiple sign-on and authentication before reaching a desired document. The Distance Education course designers and administrators were pressing for changes. There was little the library could do at that time as the library itself did not have a programmer who could design a workaround. It had to wait for either the integrated library system (Innovative Interfaces) or course management system (Blackboard) to come up with a solution to talk to each other. The adoption of EZproxy in 2007, a campus-wide initiative two years after the E-Reserve pilot, was a breakthrough in improving access to e-reserve documents within Blackboard. EZproxy is a middleware that authenticates library users against a local authentication system and provides remote access to licensed content based on the user's credentials. It was developed in 1999 by a librarian at the Maricopa Community Colleges in Arizona, United States and acquired by OCLC in January 2008. The change from authentication via the ILS to EZproxy access at Ryerson was not without wrinkles. Instructors did not know that to re-use their old materials for a new course, they had to request E-Reserve library staff to change and update the old links so that they would be compliant with the new EZproxy authentication method. Library staff did not know which course links were to be re-used and there was no global way of updating the hundreds of links in existence in many courses in Blackboard. Staff had to rely on faculty to inform them of such a need to change the links. In cases where faculty incorporated the links (created before EZproxy implementation) into their own Web pages, E-Reserve staff simply had no way of knowing about these problems until complaints from students were received. The older authentication method involved batch loading student information to enable remote access to the databases. As a result, students enrolled after 2008 did not have a login recognized by the old authentication method. When the old links were not updated, students were faced with an outdated page asking for library barcode and PIN, which they may not have handy or, in the cases of some distance education students and new students, they may not have applied for such access from the library. Circulation staff were forced to issue library barcodes, in the interim, to allow students to gain immediate access to the course readings, while waiting for E-Reserve staff to fix the links, often embedded in a long list of book and journal article titles. EZproxy also did not recognize the e-reserve account or the dummy student account. These were accounts created in Blackboard for library staff to process and check links from the student perspectives. The dummy student account was particularly useful for helping students calling from remote locations. Since these were only fake accounts that were not attached to real persons, Reserve or Reference staff were not able to go past the authentication screen to check if a link functioned from remote locations. Fortunately, this last problem was solved by the systems personnel in the Computing and Communication Services department of the university, who worked on the EZproxy project.

Not all e-reserve materials are located in the Blackboard course system. Some instructors are accustomed to the library catalogue and insist on providing access via that route. There is still demand for Print Reserve for entire books or book chapters, but the cost of obtaining copyright permissions to scan book chapters is often too high. Neither the library nor the academic departments are willing to pay for limited access. As a result, courses may have reading materials located in both Print Reserve and E-Reserve, and online readings found in both the library catalogue and Blackboard. Reference staff will have to remember these possibilities and search both locations to help students find their reading materials. There was a suggestion to run a parallel system so that materials found on the library catalogue would show in Blackboard and vice versa. Apart from being too labor intensive, the terms of access required by copyright owners (mostly publishers) also made it complicated to duplicate such links to documents in the library catalogue, without issuing individual passwords for classes. To make it easier for users and Reference staff, E-Reserve inserted a cross reference to Blackboard readings in the library catalogue, under course code or instructors.

The statistical module within Blackboard is not the most sophisticated. Ryerson E-Reserve turns on the tracking statistics module, especially for scanned articles or PDF files, some of which require copyright permission fees. The data collected results in a long list of IP addresses and a log tracking each time a page from the document was accessed, instead of the PDF document as a unit. Without the help of further programming, the statistical data was of little use. With the help of the new programmer hired by Ryerson Library in 2007, and a JAVA script to interpret the statistics, the data can now be broken down to the number of times a user with the same IP address accesses the PDF.

The Blackboard system is administered by the Office of Digital Media Projects (DMP) within the Computing and Communication Services department (CCS), which is not part of the library. DMP also maintains the server where Blackboard resides. There are pros and cons of such collaboration. The pros are that the library does not have to worry about server space, maintenance and trouble-shooting. However, as E-Reserve files start to accumulate and are not removed, access is being slowed down. To save disk space, the library is requesting a way of archiving some older files which can be retrieved easily when instructors want to re-use the same materials for new courses in later years. When problems with the Blackboard system occur, the library has to go through a middle-person – the DMP, for resolving the issues. A serious system break-down occurred in the summer of 2008 when links to documents suddenly disappeared from within folders. Back-up records were restored to provide access after some frantic efforts to diagnose the problems. Students were reminded of the feasibility of searching the library databases to retrieve some recommended readings (provided they knew what they were). Fortunately, the incident happened during the less busy part of the school year and the interruptions of service lasted for only a couple of days. As a precautionary measure, DMP did not re-activate certain tabs such as Remove for a short while, making it more labor-intensive for library E-Reserve staff to perform the same functions.

Ryerson University Library's five years of E-reserve experience within Blackboard has not been entirely smooth sailing. There is a lot of room for improvement and the time is ripe to review how the system can integrate more effectively with E-Reserve workflow and the copyright process. The E-Reserve Librarian has started to consider acquiring or creating a separate system that integrates the requesting process, the processing workflow, the copyright tracking and the display of documents for access within Blackboard. Nevertheless, Ryerson E-Reserve maintains that the choice of Blackboard to deliver course support materials is a good decision and a few thousand online courses are currently delivered via the university's learning portal. Continuing Education, including the Distance Education programs, has as many as 300–400 courses on Blackboard and the advantages and benefits of having all course-related materials in one place are undisputable. E-Reserve has enabled the library to make an initial entry into the students' virtual learning environment. The generic library tab in Blackboard for linking library resources and services was next, followed by auto-populating course-specific library content into Blackboard in 2010. Ultimately, librarians will want an increased presence in Blackboard courses, to partner with instructors in providing assistance to students in their information seeking process, and at their point of need.

4

Access and delivery of e-reserve (2)

Creative approaches – how software designed for other purposes can be adapted or utilized

Digital repositories

Lynch (2003) highlighted the changing nature of infrastructure for scholarship in the digital age:

> At any given point in time, an institutional repository will be supported by a set of information technologies, but a key part of the services that comprise an institutional repository is the management of technological changes, and the migration of digital content from one set of technologies to the next as part of the organizational commitment to providing repository services. An institutional repository is not simply a fixed set of software and hardware. (Lynch, 2003, 'Defining Institutional Repositories', para. 1)

A key finding of the CNI (Coalition for Networked Information) survey in the United States in 2003 (Lynch & Lippincott, 2005) was the significant number of IRs containing materials beyond pre-print and post-print versions of faculty research papers. Interest has surged in many institutions around the world for disseminating other types of e-content, including audio, video and images, electronic versions of graduate theses and dissertations, undergraduate student papers and multimedia projects, and ancillary evidence such as datasets, interview transcripts, etc., that might be created in the course of research, teaching, class work and cited in papers and projects (Lynch & Lippincott, 2005, 'Types of Materials in Repositories', para. 1). Confusion around the term *repository* and the management of its *digital* content arises as various groups are developing systems with the same name but serving different purposes, such as institutional (archival storage of objects) and learning object repositories (transient storage), enterprise file systems and content management systems. Libraries, and e-reserves, will have to consider the information and research cultures of their institutions before they select the type of repositories that will suit local needs.

The University of Western Australia Library gave a detailed description of their migration process of e-reserve, as a decentralized electronic collection of high-used materials, to a centralized, institution-wide electronic repository of teaching and learning materials. The Learning Resources System project was initiated to 'implement a course related materials management system that facilitates the online teaching and learning activities of the University' (Poleykett & Benn, 2003: 3). The Management and Steering Committee's members were drawn from across the university, including representatives from the University Chancellery, Student Services, the Legal Services Office, the Student Guild, faculties, and the library, which were all stakeholders in the centralized repository project. The following key components were mentioned:

- A Digital Object Repository (DOR) to store and manage the digital objects such as scanned book chapters, links to online journal articles, digital photos, audio files, or lecture notes in Microsoft Word format.
- A Resource List Management System (RLMS) sitting atop the DOR to enable students' access to an online course reading list.
- A Learning Content Management System (LCMS) as repositories which store content for use in a LMS (Learning Management System).
- A copyright management module.

Harvest Road's Hive, an Australian product, was chosen from a range of other commonly used products:

- Concord Australia Pty Ltd's Masterfile
- D-Space
- Endeavor Information Systems' ENCompass
- ExLibris' DigiTool
- FEDORA
- Harvest Road's Hive
- Intrallect's Intra Library
- The Learning Edge's The Learning Edge CMS
- WebCT Vista.

Past examination papers, scanned journal articles and book chapters in PDF and HTML documents representing links to online journal articles and Websites, were imported into the new repository from the old LMS. Some of these materials were then reassembled into reading lists. Faculty were able to submit digital material into the repository themselves or request library staff to do so on their behalf. They could manage their unit reading lists, determine their life span, organize them in the desired order or categories, and annotate each citation to inform students of its usefulness or relevancy. Utilizing the Z39.50 protocol, faculty could search the library catalogue from within the RLMS to locate a bibliographic record for an item, and pull it across. Students were able to browse or search for a single consolidated list of course materials, in electronic or print format, from the library collection. They could re-organize the list, retrieve an electronic copy and access their list of course material from WebCT, without having to log in again. According to the report, students seemed to like this user-friendly interface. Library staff also benefited from a standards-compliant repository which facilitated the management of each digital object and its copyright metadata.

Ohio State University in the United States had a pilot project, which they named as toolkit approach (Black, 2008), to integrate library resources, including e-reserve materials, into the Desire2Learn learning management system. The project made use of the Learning Object Repository (LOR) in the learning management system to store the e-reserve files, so that e-reserve staff only had to work with files in one system. Another benefit mentioned was enhanced security. Access to this section of the LOR was limited to those who worked with e-reserve except via links within the course pages in the LMS.

In terms of the software used for digital repositories, the same software that handles print materials can also be used to support audio and video formats. The ENCompass software was at one time supported by Endeavor Information Systems based in the United States, and it was one of the commercial products that had the ability to store and import or export data in eXtensible Markup Language (XML), a recognized standard for presentation of material on the Web. Its clients included the National Library of New Zealand, Cornell University, the Getty Institute in the United States, the State Library of Queensland in Australia and the Australian Commonwealth Scientific and Industrial Research Organization (ENCompass installed at 17 institutions, 2002). In 2003, Kansas State University in the United States developed a content gateway between the Virage, Inc. rich media software for managing video and related media assets and Endeavor's ENCompass digital system for managing, searching and linking collections.

Seneca College in Canada used ENCompass before 2008 (Peters-Lise, 2009). Their experience illustrated how e-reserve could be combined with a comprehensive digital collection management approach and a learning management system. Seneca College was very satisfied with ENCompass' cataloguing and display functionality. ENCompass combined the user-friendly logical browsing of their CMS (Blackboard) and the cataloguing and data control of their integrated library systems (Endeavor's Voyager). The display was more than an alphabetical list and the link was made directly to a browsable list from a course page in Blackboard.

Nevertheless, ENCompass is no longer supported by Endeavor Voyager. In 2006, Francisco Partners acquired both ExLibris and Endeavor and as a result, some of the products offered by Endeavor were phased out. In 2009, Seneca College adopted DigiTool, developed by ExLibris, to manage its digital resources and created electronic reading materials accessible through Blackboard. ExLibris is a U.S. provider of automated library solutions and DigiTool is a digital assets management system that manages and showcases digital collections. Unfortunately, there are changes being applied to DigiTool support and once again, Seneca College will have to deliberate on the next course of action.

Citation management software

The emergence of Web-based citation management (CM) software provided another opportunity for collaboration with e-reserve. There is a plethora of citation management options available today, both free and fee-based, and offered in both online and offline versions. Some of the most popular fee-based choices include: EndNote, ProCite, Reference Manager, and RefWorks. Free choices include Zotero and WizFolio.[1] All of these citation management software products offer the same basic functionality: importing citations from Websites and databases (or manually adding bibliographic information for references), which can then be manipulated by the software into bibliographies and citations in a number of different citation styles. The number of citation styles available, compatibility with vendors' proprietary databases, and additional options available vary, but the basic functionality of building a personal database of references and generating citations and bibliographies is common to all.

Citation management software offers an attractive option for faculty members. The idea of organizing one's important references in one place for their teaching and research activities is appealing, as faculty research interests tend to continue over long periods of time. Classic articles that are used and re-used in subsequent research and teaching, if stored in a personal online library, can be located and cited with the click of a button. Also a persuasive selling point is the automatic bibliography formatting option. Citation management software users do not need to learn the minutiae of the citation style they are using because the software takes care of virtually all of the formatting for them. This is a compelling reason for both students and faculty to adopt CM software, especially when they are required to format a paper in a style they have never used before. The challenge for promotion and marketing is that though faculty can often see the benefits of using this kind of software, they are reluctant or unable to devote the time necessary to learn to use it. Current users of CM software, then, are a logical target group for libraries when piloting the use of CM software for e-reserve reading lists.

The subsections below describe how citation management software can be used with CMSs to streamline the creation of e-reserve reading lists and empower faculty members to create their own lists. Both open source and fee-based examples are included, and full service, self-service, and hybrid models are considered.

How does CM software apply to e-reserve?

Submitting and filling e-reserve requests (full service model)

In a full service e-reserve model, where library staff set up e-reserve links based on faculty requests, faculty members or agents acting on their behalf submit requests to the library and the library sets the readings up for them. In this model, the following information needs to be supplied to the library's e-reserve staff: the bibliographic details for the required readings, and the class details required for systems, management or statistical record keeping purposes.

Most academic libraries offering an e-reserve service receive requests from faculty members to set up e-reserve reading lists in one or more of the following three ways: via a Web form, via an email address, or via a paper form (whether the library is utilizing a CMS/LMS, IR, or OPAC approach). If a form is the method used, the faculty member must type, cut and paste, or write by hand the course details and required bibliographic data into each field on the form. Though the control this method offers the library is beneficial in ensuring that library e-reserve staff members will have sufficient details to locate items and to set up the course readings, this field-by-field data entry can be viewed by faculty members as an unnecessary or annoying step in setting up their required reading lists. This is especially true when faculty are teaching multiple courses with long reading lists, or if they find themselves entering in details for the same readings repeatedly for different classes they are teaching. The email option, in contrast, is much more convenient for faculty, often resulting in the submission of attached Word format reading lists, course syllabi, or copied and pasted blocks of bibliographic details. The drawback of this method is that it can often create additional steps on the e-reserve staff end. The email option offers no control for requiring specific pieces of information (as a Web form can) and it is easier for the person submitting the request to miss a required piece of information than when given a form, complete with required fields, to follow.

For faculty members already using citation management software, both the library and faculty members can potentially benefit from its addition or replacement as the avenue for creating electronic reading lists.

Because citation management software can receive metadata directly from the library's subscribed indexing and full text databases, there is a certain amount of quality control built in to the process.[2] Further, in cases where no citation was located and the manual entry option is chosen, the CM software employs a form composed of bibliographic metadata fields so that users are guided to input all of the required metadata that staff require to locate the item(s). Additionally, most citations sent from databases to the CM product include a URL and/or a database or vendor name, which is added to appropriate fields for that citation in the CM software. Because the database name or URL is included, this can potentially save staff time in locating a full text version of the items to be placed on e-reserve. In this way, the fields and required bibliographic metadata that e-reserve administrators are accustomed to requiring on Web and paper electronic reading list request forms are already built in to CM software. The benefit of this is twofold: faculty efforts are minimized when they do not need to re-key bibliographic details, and staff members' work is reduced as the step of checking the accuracy of citations and hunting for missing bits of citation information is virtually eliminated.

The remaining parts of the equation in setting up reading lists using citation management software are: conveying the course details that the library may require for systems or management reasons (i.e. course code, instructor name, number of students, class start and end dates, or copyright clearance requests), and the method of getting the data from the CM software to the appropriate library staff members. A potential drawback of the citation management software approach to e-reserve is that the methods for filling in these portions of the equation may not be obvious to faculty. Because of this, library staff involved in promoting the service and in informing faculty members of the procedures require straightforward instructions, and enticing marketing materials in order to get faculty interested in and comfortable with this option. At virtually all institutions promoting CM software as a method of creating reading lists, this is presented as one of a few available methods – an exception to this discovered by the authors is Nipissing University in North Bay, Canada (discussed below). Unless the citation management software approach is the only available option presented to faculty members for creating e-reserve reading lists, gaining faculty buy-in is a vital consideration, and marketing and instructions are necessary ingredients for faculty participation.

Fee-based example: RefWorks and Blackboard

RefWorks is a Web-based bibliographic citation manager that allows users to collect, save and organize bibliographic citations to journal articles, books, Websites and other sources that were found during research. With it users can create correctly formatted bibliographies in the style of their choice (RefWorks-COS, 2009a).

RefWorks building block

In conjunction with Northwestern University in the United States, Blackboard created an open-source building block or RefWorks Bridge Extension allowing Blackboard customers to provide one-click access from Blackboard to RefWorks databases (RefWorks-COS, 2009b). This allows the two systems to talk to one another, so that records saved in RefWorks by faculty members can be displayed within Blackboard as course reading lists. In order to utilize this option, the RefWorks administrator, generally one or more of the institution's librarians, must provide the Blackboard administrator, usually a campus computing or equivalent department staff member, with the RefWorks administrator username and password. Because the administrator login and password can be used for customization and permission setting activities for the institution's RefWorks accounts, this may or may not be an attractive option. On the positive side, once the Blackboard and RefWorks administrators set up the building block, the process of generating course reading lists using the RefWorks option within Blackboard is very intuitive.

Once the building block has been installed, instructors can access their own RefWorks account(s) from within their Blackboard course tools area (refer to Figure 4.1). When a faculty member selects the RefWorks course tool, they are prompted to choose to link to an account they already have set up, or to create a new RefWorks account to be used for that course. Students will be able to see all of the different folders that the RefWorks account creator has set up, and can use OpenURL buttons to link out to electronic versions of the readings. RefWorks employs a folder structure, so that the RefWorks account linked to the Blackboard course can have different folders for weekly readings, for specific themes, or any other organization the instructor wishes to use.

Figure 4.1   RefWorks Course Tool

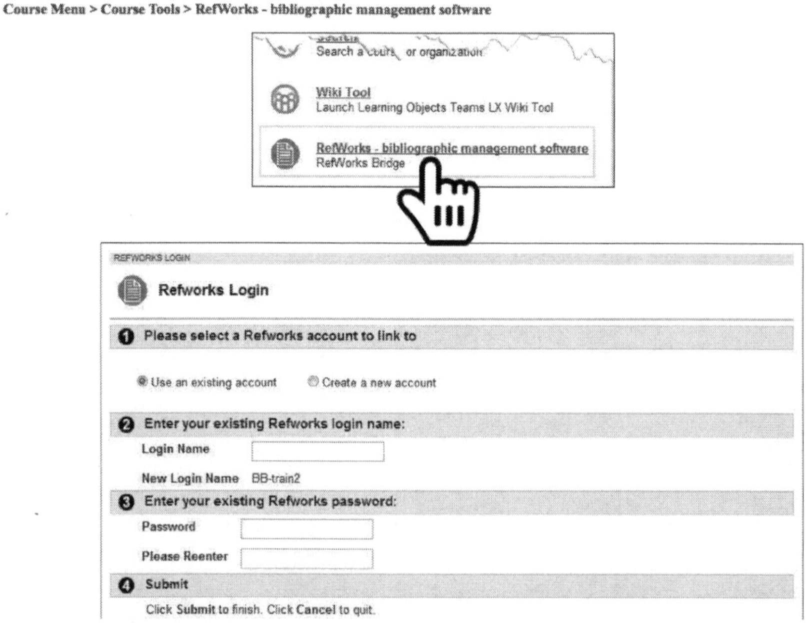

Course Menu > Course Tools > RefWorks – bibliographic management software

Adapted from Worcester Polytechnic Institute Academic Technology Center, Refworks: The Citation Management tool. http://www.wpi.edu/Academics/ATC/Collaboratory/How To/ MyWPI/refworks.html

Figure 4.2   RefWorks Organize Folders area

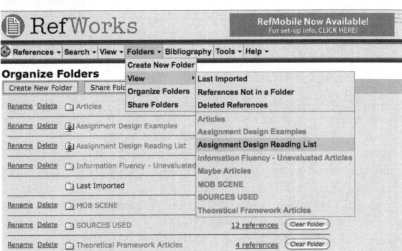

If the faculty member chooses to create a read-only password for their account, students can be automatically logged in to this read-only version from Blackboard and cannot edit, add or delete information from the RefWorks account. Instructors also have the option of automatically logging their students into their regular account from Blackboard, which may be desirable when a collaborative approach to the course is taken. Because RefWorks administrators can allow authorized users to create an unlimited number of RefWorks accounts, faculty could have the option to create a separate account for each course they teach. RefWorks account data can be easily copied from one account to another, so that a faculty member could use a master account to create all course reference lists, and then could set up separate accounts for each group of course-specific resources.

The RefWorks building block makes sense within a self-serve model, because faculty members have a simple, obvious option for integrating RefWorks reading lists into their Blackboard course material. Another reason the building block easily enables faculty to create their own electronic reading lists is the inclusion of OpenURL links that are automatically associated with each reference in RefWorks. The institution's RefWorks administrator can specify relevant details about the institution's link resolver so that OpenURL buttons, icons, or links will display beside each reference within the software for all of that institution's RefWorks accounts. The automatic inclusion of an OpenURL link associated with each reference means that neither library staff members nor faculty need worry about searching for the item and obtaining a persistent URL. Using OpenURL, the full text options available to the user are those that are available to that particular user and at that specific moment in time. Faculty members do not need to contact e-reserve or other library staff unless the readings are not online, or there is a problem with the OpenURL links.

A hybrid or full service model could also work with the RefWorks building block. E-reserve staff could set up RefWorks accounts and add items on behalf of the faculty member, and could then supply the full account or *read only* account details to the faculty member for linking their Blackboard course with RefWorks readings. This would not streamline the process of setting up the e-reserve list, but would still offer the benefits of full citation details and flexible organization of the materials over other Blackboard e-reserve linking options. Faculty who had built their own RefWorks account, but who wish to have the OpenURL links checked by library staff could supply their login details and staff could recommend any changes, or if full login details were provided, make any necessary adjustments to the links (see the sections below for some work-around solutions being utilized to bypass RefWorks OpenURLs to prefer persistent links).

Figure 4.3	**RefWorks database view. Get it! @ Ryerson Buttons are Ryerson University's SFX OpenURL link resolver service**

Figure 4.4 **SFX menu view showing full text and help services available for a citation from RefWorks**

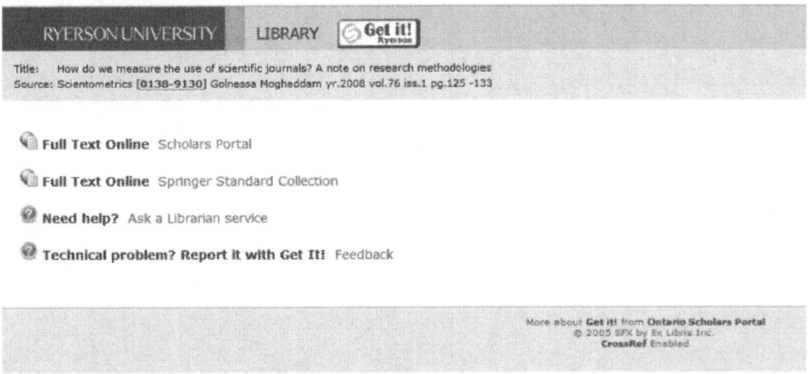

Copyright Ex Libris Ltd. Used by permission.

A number of American academic libraries have used the RefWorks Blackboard building block, including Northwestern University, Cornell, University of South Florida, University of North Florida, and Princeton. Outside the U.S., Queensland University in Australia and the City University of Hong Kong have also implemented the building block. City University of Hong Kong (Run Run Shaw Library, City University of Hong Kong, 2007) has created an excellent instructional video illustrating the process of accessing the RefWorks e-reserve readings by students. The video also demonstrates the SFX OpenURL linking method from RefWorks in Blackboard.

RefShare

Another method of generating course reading lists in Blackboard based on RefWorks databases is through the use of RefShare. RefShare is an optional add-on for RefWorks subscribers available at an additional cost. This option does not require the installation of a building block, and the library RefWorks administrator does not need to divulge their administrator login and password. With RefShare, RefWorks users can choose to create links to folders of references, individual references, or an entire RefWorks database that can be shared with colleagues or students via email delivery or display on any Web, wiki, or blog page. Note that this is another difference from the RefWorks building block, as with the building block, the entire account, all folders and references, is always displayed in Blackboard. The RefShare link is created using a share folder or share database button, which leads the user to a page displaying the RefShare link and an option to email the RefShare URL to specific individual(s). This link can also simply be copied and pasted within a Web page. Various view, export, and collaboration options can be enabled or disabled by the RefWorks account holder to determine what the individual or group (with whom the sharer is sharing) is permitted to do with the shared items. The RefWorks account holder can limit access, view, and download permissions to these folders or items so that students can be allowed only to view references and link to full text versions, or to permit students to create bibliographies and export items to their own RefWorks accounts. Comments or notes can be permitted at the item (i.e. book or journal article) level so that students can be encouraged to share impressions and comments related to the readings with their instructor and classmates. The link created goes to RefShare, a RefWorks-like environment that can be accessed by anyone who has the link. A faculty member or e-reserve staff member could add a RefShare URL to a CMS and when students click on that link, they get to the RefShare view of that item or list. The OpenURL links then, as with the RefWorks building block, facilitate linking to full text items. RefShare can also be a good

Figure 4.5 — RefWork RefShare option to Share References displays all folders available. Share Folder buttons go to the sharing options for that folder, and Share Entire Database is an available choice

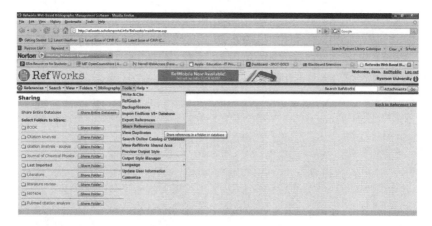

Figure 4.6

RefShare view of a shared RefWorks folder.
Note that edit and delete options available in
RefWorks are not available in RefShare

Figure 4.7

RefShare Shared Folder Options. Permissions
are set, the URL is displayed, and additional
information can be added

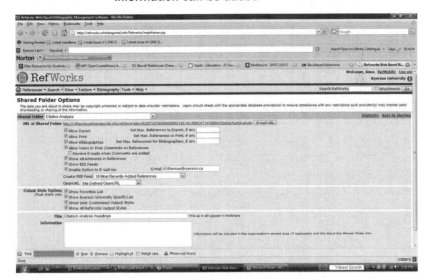

way to facilitate group projects via shared folders for storing research online. Because RefWorks also includes an attachment feature that can be set up to display attachments in RefShare, full text documents that have cleared copyright may be uploaded to the RefWorks server and attached to the corresponding citation in RefWorks. This is done with an upload option similar to attaching a file to an email. RefShare links may be shared with members of the general public, but as long as the links are not shared beyond the instructor and those enrolled in the course on Blackboard, the institution may use this option without the danger of unauthorized access.

Examples of libraries offering RefShare for e-reserve

Ryerson University pilot project

Ryerson University in Toronto, Canada is part of a consortium of 21 Ontario college and university libraries. In 2004, the Ontario Council of University Libraries (OCUL) signed on to license CSA's (now ProQuest's) RefWorks. Adoption was somewhat slow getting started, but by 2006 the number of accounts at Ryerson alone had grown to 9,110. Now, on average, 321 new users are accessing RefWorks each month, and there are 576 faculty accounts. In addition to this growing user base, the librarians are aware that there are also a number of faculty members at Ryerson who are Endnote users. Because Endnote libraries can be easily imported into RefWorks, those faculty members could add their Endnote libraries to RefWorks for use as e-reserve reading lists with minimal effort (RefWorks-COS, 2009c).

In 2007, the Digital Support and E-Reserve Librarians began planning a pilot project utilizing RefWorks for e-reserve. E-reserve volume had been continually increasing, and it was thought at that time that RefWorks could be a good option for saving staff time and empowering faculty to create and manage their own e-reserves. The software was identified because of the automatic inclusion of OpenURLs, which the library had already begun using as one of the linking methods from Blackboard e-reserve lists, and because faculty members were known to be using the RefWorks citation manager already.

In 2007, the relationship with Computing and Communication Services (CCS) was not ideal for implementing the Blackboard building block quickly or easily. RefShare was a more attractive option than the RefWorks building block because it required no additional product installations. To begin, the Digital Support Librarian used Excel to compare active RefWorks user account email addresses with a list of email addresses from the faculty directory. The overlapping email addresses were then compared with a list of past e-reserve users. The findings indicated that the Nursing faculty would be an appropriate group to approach for a pilot project because several individuals from this faculty were present on both lists. The Digital Support and E-Reserve Librarians met with the Nursing Liaison Librarian to discuss whether the faculty members identified as having both RefWorks and e-reserve experience in this department would be amenable to participating in the pilot project.

To market the pilot, the Digital Support Librarian created two videos using screen and audio capture software called *Camtasia*, which the library had previously licensed for producing in-house instructional videos. One video, entitled *RefWorks: Easy as 1,2,3* (Thomas, 2007a), illustrated in 2 minutes how RefWorks can be used to store research, organize it, and produce bibliographies. A similar video, *RefShare: Easy as 1,2,3* (Thomas, 2007b), demonstrated how RefWorks/RefShare can be used to create reading lists in Blackboard in 3 steps: 1 share your folder, 2 copy the link, and 3 paste it into Blackboard.

The Digital Support and E-Reserve Librarians created an invitation in MS Word document format which included a description of the anticipated benefits: faculty control over reading lists, flexible organization and formatting of lists, support of academic integrity, and not having to wait for library staff to set up the list. Also included in this document were links to the two videos described above, and assurance that if faculty members chose to participate in this pilot, they would still have full support from the library. With assistance from the Nursing Liaison Librarian, this Word document was emailed to the School of Nursing.

There were no responses to the initial invitation, so the E-Reserve and Digital Support Librarians decided that more marketing and a wider target group was needed in order to get the pilot going. It is possible that the documentation emailed was enough information for faculty to create their own RefShare shared reading lists and that they did not require assistance from the library, but it is more likely that this was not adequate promotion to generate interest, and none of these faculty members decided to use this option for e-reserve.

Later efforts employed to generate interest included the Lunch and Learn presentations given in conjunction with the university's Digital Media Projects Office wherein the Blackboard administrator, E-Reserve Librarian, and Digital Support Librarian illustrated RefShare as an exciting new way to create e-reserve reading lists in Blackboard. Another tactic employed was to include the Word document invitation in a flyer provided to new faculty as part of their orientation packet. These efforts have to date not been successful, unless faculty are sharing lists on their own without the library's knowledge. Again, it is possible that individual faculty members are doing this, but library staff have not seen evidence of this within Blackboard courses to which the library has access.

The authors hypothesize that there are a few barriers preventing the success of this pilot project. First, the *self service* model promoted may not be seen as an advantage among faculty members. Though it takes longer for the library to generate reading lists in Blackboard, it still may be more attractive to just let the library take care of this task rather than to learn to use a new method. Second, faculty members may not like the OpenURL linking method for e-reserve. Because our E-Reserve department will generate persistent links to full text articles, and the OpenURL linking levels vary from the article level to database level, the linking may not meet faculty or student expectations (see Chapter 6 for more about linking and OpenURL). Third, current RefWorks users do not necessarily use RefShare. The need to share a folder, copy the link, and paste it into Blackboard may be seen as too much work, so that the older method is preferred.

Since the Ryerson pilot plan was initiated based on staff need, and the drawbacks of standard Blackboard linking do not create a lot of problems for faculty or students, the authors feel that more dialogue with faculty is needed to assess whether this method would address their needs better than the alternatives. Another possibility discussed is the need for more effective and intensive promotion of the service, illustrating the ease of use and anticipated benefits for students and faculty. The authors hypothesize that enabling the *DirectLink* feature for SFX (discussed in Chapter 6 below) and utilizing RefWorks' attachment feature for uploading scanned articles, combined with increased promotion and dialogue with faculty, will generate more interest and participation in this option.

Nipissing University – self-serve model

Nipissing University is located in North Bay, Ontario, Canada and serves a population of 5,235 full time equivalent students (FTE). The university employs Blackboard for online course management. The Education Centre Library serves both Nipissing University and Canadore College, and does not describe their library as utilizing an e-reserve system per se. With the acquisition of RefShare, the Library began providing instructions for faculty on how to set up electronic reading lists using RefShare (Innerd, 2009). Faculty create a RefWorks folder for their course containing the citations for their readings, and then share the folder using RefShare. These are provided to the student in two ways: via the RefShare URL in Blackboard, and within the Education Centre Library's RefShare area, accessible via the Library's Website at *http://www.eclibrary.ca/library/ library-information-mainmenu-275/for-faculty-mainmenu-60/ refworksrefshare*. Interested readers can view their RefShare area at *http://refworks.scholarsportal.info/refshare/?site=010141091228080000*, but should note that the SFX links to subscribed resources require an active Canadore or Nippissing student, faculty, or staff account. Some faculty do not use Blackboard and prefer instead to include a RefShare link on their own Website. Students then use the Library's SFX OpenURL link resolver to connect to articles listed in RefShare.

Using RefShare for electronic reading lists was first encouraged in the autumn of 2007, when the Education Centre Library gained access to RefShare. Access became available too late to do any real promotion that academic year, but the following year (2008–9) the service was expanded through word of mouth and in collaboration with the Faculty and Administrative Support Services (FASS). That year FASS created and shared folders on behalf of faculty, and the librarians answered their questions and provided training to faculty who wanted to create and share folders on their own. The other jumpstart for using RefShare was a strong collaboration with the Inservice and Continuing Education departments. Inservice offers continuing education courses for teachers, and both departments saw RefWorks and RefShare as a way to manage references more easily and to facilitate the move to online course materials. In so doing, they were able to get rid of print course packs and the need to mail those out.

Currently, the librarians do not create folders for faculty. FASS were reorganized in 2009 and are maintaining existing folders, but are no longer creating folders. Innerd feels that the use is growing as more faculty are using RefWorks and she reported users commenting that they heard about it and asked if she could show them how to create an electronic reading list with RefShare. At one point Innerd ran some open sessions on using RefShare that included faculty attendance. These open sessions proved to be a really useful way to talk about other things regarding the library.

The Education Centre Library chose to use RefShare for reading lists because it was an available way to provide access to course materials without having to invest in a true e-reserves system. The Education Centre's librarians report that it has been working fairly well and with positive feedback. Because for the most part it is done by the faculty themselves, the librarians tend to only hear when there are problems. The librarians note that there are many faculty using it that they do not hear from at all. Librarians do their best to solve any technical problems that come up. Innerd also created a presentation which she posted and advertised to the faculty, and she knows of at least one instance of a faculty member who, after viewing the presentation, was able to use RefShare successfully for a course without any contact with the library.

Though the library reports both positive feedback and faculty uptake, this project has not been without its hiccups. Because RefWorks and RefShare were not designed for e-reserves, some problems have come up that the librarians have had to address. For example, some journals provide selected articles for free, and sometimes Websites are the desired content type that faculty want to include on reading lists for students. RefWorks and RefShare automatically display an SFX button beside each reference, and also include a URL field. SFX contains information about an institution's holdings and free journals, but not Websites, many electronic books, and other non-journal content. Because of this, individual free e-journal articles and other content types available online were not linkable through SFX. In addition, linking levels vary from the database level to the article level, so that students were not always able to get close enough to their article to easily locate it using SFX.

As an interim solution to this problem, students were given instructions indicating which readings to get to via the SFX button and which readings to access using the URL field. Persistent links were added to the URL field in RefWorks and were displayed to students as hyperlinks alongside each reference. This was not an ideal solution, as students would see both a hyperlink and a Get it! button for each reference and needed to consult instructions before knowing which to choose.

More recently, Geoff Sinclair, Nipissing's Manager of Technical Services, created and shared a solution to modify SFX's handling of RefWorks OpenURLs (Sinclair, 2009). In the event that SFX does not translate the OpenURL sent by RefWorks into an acceptable URL for the resource, a persistent link to the article is added within square brackets into the reference title field in RefWorks. With Sinclair's work-around for SFX in place, the persistent URL added to the title field in RefWorks is used by SFX instead of the link SFX would otherwise create based on Nipissing's online collections activated in SFX. Because SFX will use the persistent link whenever it is in the reference title in RefWorks, students can now utilize the SFX button exclusively. Sinclair's solution has eliminated the need to sometimes click on the SFX button and sometimes click on a hyperlink. This has created a more consistent experience for the students.

Another recent improvement for student access was gained by implementing a single sign-on integration from Blackboard to RefShare. EZproxy is used to eliminate a second login for electronic resources. The students log in to Blackboard, and EZproxy then recognizes the course management domain using an HTTP referrer [sic] header. This improvement was especially beneficial for the students, as the credentials for the CMS and the proxy server are not the same.

Despite Sinclair's persistent URL solution and single sign-on, the linking from Blackboard is still not universally done using RefShare. Some materials, sample papers for example, are uploaded directly to Blackboard, and some links to publicly available Websites are in Blackboard areas other than the RefShare reading lists. Sinclair feels that forcing course designers and faculty to always use RefShare for course readings is neither possible nor necessarily desirable. The librarians noted a recent case illustrating this, in which non-library staff responsible for course management design had linked to a publicly available journal article, rather than using a subscription-based database. After attempting to create a link to the article within RefWorks, the librarians determined that the database vendor provided journal-level resolution of OpenURL links for that resource. The librarians could hardly blame the designer for selecting the direct link to the publicly available article in this situation. Another reason that direct links within Blackboard may be preferred over the RefShare method is the variability in the source data transferred from the database vendor to RefWorks. Sometimes when references are exported from vendors to RefWorks, the vendor's export function processed by the RefWorks import filter produces a result that is not ideal for OpenURL linking. Because of the export/import transition from vendor to RefWorks, the data used to build the OpenURL at the vendor's site may not be the same data used to build the OpenURL within RefWorks.

The Education Centre Library's experience illustrates how the creative use of software for e-reserve designed for a different purpose can require tweaking to deliver easy access for students. It also shows that CM software has limitations and inconsistencies in terms of linking. Collaboration with other departments, faculty empowerment, and savings in staff time gained by eliminating print reserve mailings are positive outcomes, but new demands on staff time can arise when addressing technical issues and formulating work-arounds.

York University – full service model

York University is located in North Toronto, Ontario, Canada, and serves a much larger population than either Ryerson or Nipissing, at 45,259 full time equivalents (FTE).

At an e-reserve forum at University of Guelph-Humber in July 2009, Laura Walton from York University described York's use of RefWorks for e-reserve. York is currently utilizing RefShare to improve access to electronic reading lists for distance education masters nursing students (Walton, 2009). These students have varying degrees of computer literacy, and the York Library catalogue display for their readings was proving difficult for them to navigate. The course reading lists given to the students by their instructor were broken down into various modules, with readings in each module in APA format, sorted alphabetically by author last name. York's library catalogue was unable to display the items on e-reserve in a similar fashion. The catalogue list was sorted by title, and students were finding it difficult to locate the alphabetically sorted readings for each module in this single, title-sorted list.

In this case, RefShare was well suited to the students' needs. The model chosen at York was to provide the full service. Walton set up the RefWorks accounts and corresponding references on behalf of the instructors, and created folders to mimic the modules on the students' reading lists. In the library catalogue, RefShare links were added to the 856 (link) MARC field, and the items were described according to the course and module information. This way, the students are able to quickly find the module they are working on in York's catalogue, and link to the RefShare folder containing the readings for that module. At RefShare, the readings are automatically sorted by author last name, so they are in the same order as on the students' lists.

Walton's e-reserve solution did not end here. She decided not to have the students utilize the SFX OpenURLs for Find it! @ York. Instead, she includes persistent URLs to the article level within the article source field, and when the articles' reference type is set to *Journal, Electronic* in RefWorks, the persistent URL is displayed beneath the citation information, and is hyperlinked. Students use this link to connect to their readings instead of clicking on the Find it! @ York. Here, Walton utilized a more low-tech approach than was employed at the Education Centre Library to address a similar problem. The philosophy behind this decision is that students should be taken directly to their required readings, rather than be presented with a menu of choices. The SFX Open URL linking level variation and the additional step of choosing an option from a menu conflicts with this philosophy. Walton was able to use a simple fix to achieve persistent linking with RefShare.

At York, RefShare met an acute need expressed by students, and has therefore been successful.

Simon Fraser University (SFU) – RefShare as one of a few options

Simon Fraser University (SFU) is located in Burnaby and Surrey, British Columbia, Canada and serves a student population of approximately 25,000 FTE. The SFU Library's page providing information for faculty on creating required reading lists includes several different methods (Groves, 2009). The e-reserve access points recommended are: through the library catalogue, from WebCT via persistent links, and from WebCT via RefShare OpenURLs. Each method includes a description of associated benefits and cautions. Based on the information provided on their Website, the authors understand that SFU is offering a full e-reserve service only for the library catalogue option. Both the WebCT persistent linking, and WebCT linking via RefShare and OpenURL are presented as self-service options (faculty create the RefWorks list or persistent URLs themselves following the library's instructions). The cautions they advertised against the full service catalogue option include: the addition of an extra step when faculty need to submit their request to library staff, and the limit on organization of readings in the catalogue to the order that the requests are processed. RefShare is cautioned because not all desired readings will have online versions that can be linked to through OpenURL, and also because faculty will need to check the OpenURL links periodically to see if the library still has access to the resources. The primary benefit described for the catalogue method is that links are verified and maintained by library staff. Another benefit presented for the catalogue option is that staff have already addressed copyright.

RefWorks without the building block

Even without the use of the building block or RefShare, RefWorks could be used on its own with Blackboard and other CMSs. The bibliography creation option in RefWorks includes HTML as an available format. HTML is also a common format that can be used to add content and information to a CMS. For institutions subscribing to RefWorks that do not wish to install the building block, nor subscribe to RefShare, it is still possible to create RefWorks reading lists within Blackboard in the following way. Step one, build your RefWorks database. Step two, click on the bibliography menu. Step three, choose your *output style*, HTML format type, and the folder of your required readings. Step four, click *create bibliography*.

Figure 4.8 RefWorks bibliography creation options

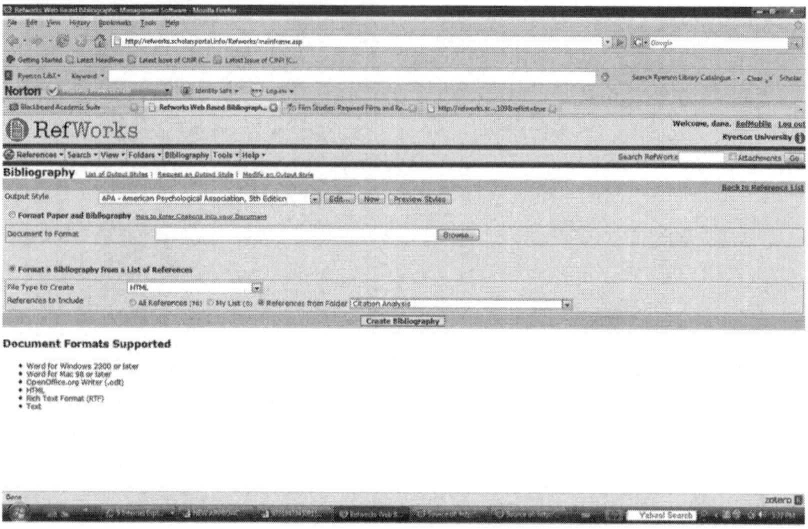

Image published with permission of ProQuest LLC © 2009 ProQuest LLC; all rights reserved. Further reproduction prohibited without permission.

Step five, view the page source information with the appropriate browser option.

Step six, paste the HTML code copied in step six into the HTML editor for Blackboard at the desired location.

Voila!

RefWorks administrators have the option of creating customized citation styles that they may make available for all RefWorks users at their institution (RefWorks-COS, 2009d). This is notable because of the recent RefWorks update that enabled the inclusion of the OpenURL as a field in bibliographic entries. At Ryerson University, the administrator has created a citation style called E-RESERVE APA. When faculty members create a bibliography in this style, the OpenURL is automatically included below the full metadata for each reading on their list.

Figure 4.9

RefWorks APA bibliography in HTML format. Pop-up window displays the page source for copying the HTML

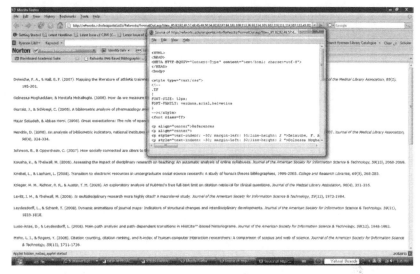

Figure 4.10

Blackboard content creation. Source code from previous figure pasted into the HTML text editor

Figure 4.11 Blackboard display of the pasted reading list

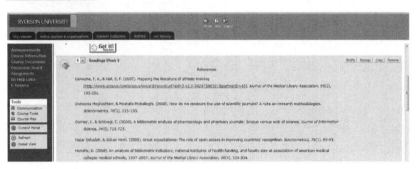

Figure 4.12 RefWorks Bibliography Creation option showing E-RESERVE APA customized citation style

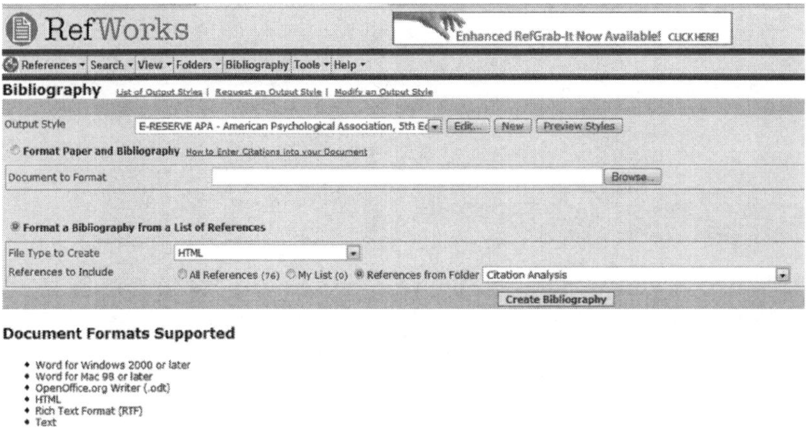

Another method of adding links to the readings within a RefWorks bibliography is to use an HTML export option utilizing a citation style that adds the URL or links field to the end of every reference type. This would take whatever information that is in that URL or links field and display it at the end of each reference. The drawback with this approach is that the individual working with the reading list in RefWorks would need to ensure that this link or URL is persistent, and if it is a subscribed resource, that the institution's authentication method was utilized. The OpenURL option described above is more realistic for faculty to employ themselves, as the task of creating an appropriate link can be complex (see Chapter 6 for more details on linking).

Figure 4.13

RefWorks bibliography in E-RESERVE APA style. URLs below each bibliographic entry are SFX OpenURL links

Image published with permission of ProQuest LLC © 2009 ProQuest LLC; all rights reserved. Further reproduction prohibited without permission.

Figure 4.14 RefShare view of a shared RefWorks folder

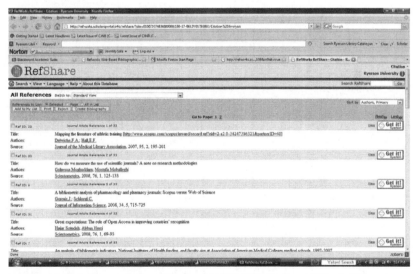

Image published with permission of ProQuest LLC © 2009 ProQuest LLC; all rights reserved. Further reproduction prohibited without permission.

Benefits of the citation management approach

Speed and empowerment (self-serve model)

E-reserve departments in academic libraries usually receive high request volume in August, September, December and January. Faculty members can often underestimate the time needed by library staff to set up e-reserve reading lists for them, and this can cause delays for students in obtaining access to their readings. In cases where copyright clearance is required, it is difficult to control this. However, where required readings are already available online to the institution's authorized users, the process of creating e-reserve lists can be done quickly. The citation management software options described above can be done entirely by faculty members unless they require assistance with linking or help in using the citation management software. Current RefWorks users can use their accounts to generate reading lists that are already linked with the library's resources via OpenURL. This way, the control over the list rests entirely with the faculty, and they are able to set up the e-reserve readings whenever they wish, rather than waiting for the library to do this for them. Changes made to the RefWorks account will then automatically update the Blackboard reading list (if using either the Blackboard building block or RefShare methods), because Blackboard lists access RefWorks and RefShare dynamically every time users select those lists.

Additional benefits for students and staff

Use of the RefWorks Blackboard building block or RefShare within Blackboard can help institutions support student academic integrity. Plagiarism due to incomplete or improperly referenced sources is a form that some undergraduate students fail to recognize (Roig, 1997). RefWorks and RefShare reading lists can be set up to display in any of the over 900 citation styles available in RefWorks. The Blackboard resource description is very limited in terms of the number of characters that can be used, and the use of italics and other symbols is not available. Because of this, a complete citation to the resources on e-reserve is not possible with standard Blackboard external links. RefWorks accounts can be customized to add citation style views that can be selected using a 'switch to' view pull down menu.

RefWorks, RefShare, and Blackboard together make it possible to display reading lists in the citation style that students will need to use for their own writing assignments. This provides an excellent opportunity to give citation examples to students to point to when discussing assignment

Figure 4.15 RefWorks Switch View options

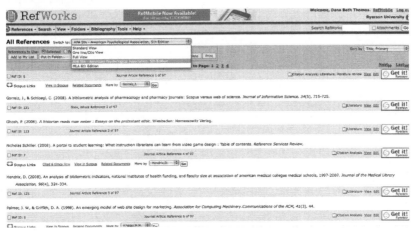

writing guidelines and academic integrity. Also, using RefWorks for reading lists provides some familiarity for the students with the use of Citation Management software, so that they may be more inclined to learn how to use it to format their bibliographies for their essays.

The complete citation information that RefWorks and RefShare provide for Blackboard e-reserve reading lists also provides a benefit for staff members. Because of the changeable nature of electronic resources, various technical problems can occur which prevent seamless linking. When linking problems occur, and full citation information is available, the item can be easily looked up and perhaps located through an alternate route. However, if only an article title is provided, it becomes much harder to locate that item. When students cannot link to their readings, and go to the library for help, the options for staff members to troubleshoot Blackboard links used to be limited to Googling the article title, or trying numerous databases based on the subject matter suggested by the title. This was a frustrating exercise for both parties.

Open source examples

Sakai and Citations Helper

An interesting project to watch is the Mellon Foundation funded, Integrating Licensed Library Resources with Sakai. This project, also known as Sakaibrary (Indiana University Digital Library Program, 2008) was carried out by Indiana University and University of Michigan in partnership with Johns Hopkins University, Northwestern University, Stanford University, and the University of California–Berkeley in the United States. Recognizing that adding links to institutionally licensed electronic resources in the CMS was difficult for faculty to accomplish, the Sakaibrary team worked on creating a tool for Sakai that would make this process more user friendly. They came up with a tool that they named Citations Helper that enabled users to add citation information including persistent URLs from library databases, metasearch engines and Google Scholar to reading lists in the Sakai CMS. Citations Helper also includes an option to add lists of citations from citation management software like Zotero and RefWorks. The project discovered some limitations with the Citations Helper application due to differences across vendor databases and problems retrieving reliable durable URLs, and so utilized OpenURLs instead for linking. Despite the limitations of the new tool, the fact that it was not enabled by default in the Sakai course tools, and was not being widely advertised at Indiana University, the result was still that 'the instructors of 51 courses elected to use Citations Helper during the fall 2007 semester, and 49 used it during the spring 2008 semester' (Dun & Hollar, 2008: 8). Similarly, at the University of Michigan:

> in the fall 2007 semester, the instructors of 45 courses enabled the Citations Helper feature, and in the winter 2008 semester, the instructors of 30 courses enabled the feature. In addition, the owners of 68 project sites have enabled Citations Helper, and 95 individual users have enabled it in their personal workspaces. (Dun & Hollar, 2008: 9)

There are two demo sites for Sakaibrary that can be used to test the Citation Helper, located at *http://www.dlib.indiana.edu/projects/sakai/demo/*.

Zotero

A simple way to implement citation management software for e-reserve without paying for software or developing an in-house tool like Citations Helper is to utilize open source options as is. However, as illustrated below, links are not as easy or straightforward to include as with other citation management options described above. Because of this, a full-service or hybrid model rather than a self-service model would be more appropriate unless faculty members at the institution are very savvy with linking and understand the nature of the library's electronic resources and authentication method(s).

Zotero is an open source citation management software extension available for the Mozilla Firefox browser. References can be imported from databases and Websites to one's Zotero library that can be used to create reports and bibliographies in HTML and other formats. Interested readers can download both the Firefox browser (*http://www.mozilla. com/*) and the Zotero extension (*https://addons.mozilla.org/en-US/ firefox/addon/3504*) for free. To generate a bibliography or report of items in one's Zotero library, one highlights item(s) required for readings, and right clicks to choose to create the bibliography. On the next screen, the user can then choose the HTML format.

Figure 4.16   **Zotero library view showing options to create HTML bibliography or report file from a list of items in your library**

Figure 4.17   **Zotero HTML bibliography file shown with Zotero library frame beneath**

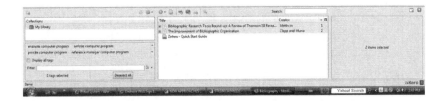

When using the Firefox browser, an OpenURL link resolver can be recognized through COinS (Context Object in Spans). If this bibliography is pasted into an online course page and then viewed with the Firefox browser, the OpenURL button will also show up because of COinS, but will not show up if viewed with the more popular Internet Explorer browser.

Figure 4.18 Example Report created by Zotero that can be saved as an HTML file. Note that bibliographic details as well as the database of origin (JSTOR) and URL are included

The Improvement of Bibliographic Organization

Type	Journal Article
Author	Verner W. Clapp
Author	Kathrine O. Murra
Publication	The Library Quarterly
Volume	25
Issue	1
Pages	91-110
Date	Jan., 1955
DOI	10.2307/4304386
ISSN	00242519
URL	http://www.jstor.org.ezproxy.lib.ryerson.ca/stable/4304386
Accessed	June-02-09 1:56:00 PM
Repository	JSTOR
Extra	ArticleType: primary_article / Full publication date: Jan., 1955 / Copyright © 1955 The University of Chicago Press
Date Added	June-02-09 1:56:00 PM
Modified	June-02-09 1:56:00 PM

Attachments

JSTOR: The Library Quarterly, Vol. 25, No. 1 (Jan., 1955), pp. 91-110
The Improvement of Bibliographic Organization

When HTML files created from the Zotero export options are viewed as page source, the HTML code can be copied and pasted using the HTML format option. If the library staff are not comfortable with HTML, this can also be accomplished copying and pasting from the regular browser display to a WSYWIG (what-you-see-is-what-you-get) editor, but there may be formatting issues that need to be cleaned up if this is the chosen workflow.

Because the OpenURLs only appear with the Firefox browser, a more consistent way to include links is needed. If an OpenURL link is desired, one may change Zotero preferences to recognize the institution's OpenURL link resolver. This preference selects the OpenURL service to be used as Zotero's locate option. Once this is set up, e-reserve links can be added by copying the OpenURL links for each article and pasting those into the URL field within Zotero for each citation. The other option is to use the locate button within Zotero to view online sources for the items, and utilize persistent linking options (with the proxy rewrite) offered by vendors to update the Zotero URL field. The bibliography preference can be altered to include the URL information for each reference.

Zotero groups offers another avenue for creating online reading lists.

Figure 4.19 Firefox Browser display of an SFX menu for a journal article. The Zotero window is at the bottom frame of the browser

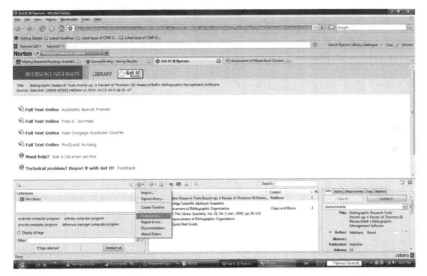

Copyright Ex Libris Ltd. Used by permission.

Zotero account holders can add items or folders of items from their Zotero libraries to the Zotero groups Website. The site is public and is searchable, but group libraries can be made either public or private. Zotero includes an option to add files to associated references, but only references, not these associated files, are visible on groups. Private groups can be created, and the group owner then invites others to join. Group members can be assigned different levels of access, such as view only, view, edit and add information. In addition to citation information, notes, identification of group members, and other information can be shared in Zotero groups. For faculty and students with mobile devices, it is beneficial that sharing to groups remotely is also possible. See as an example of a public group English 478 (*http://www.zotero.org/groups/english_478_shakespeare_ and_the_modern_world*). In terms of flexibility for pointing students to

Figure 4.20 Zotero preferences showing the option to add the OpenURL link Resolver

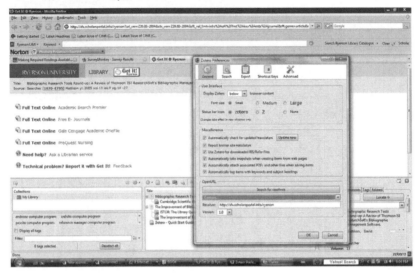

Figure 4.21 Zotero groups

particular sections of a Zotero group, it is simple to copy and paste a link to any area within the group. The group, group library, individual folders, and individual items within folders may all be linked to by copying and pasting the URL that displays in the browser's address bar, or when mousing over that item. Folders and subfolders may be created to organize content. The folders are a nice option, but Zotero groups also presents a content display limitation. Items within groups are displayed as they are added, and cannot be sorted according to other desired criteria. This means that most recently added items display at the top of any list, and items added previously are funneled to the bottom.

Amherst College in Massachusetts, United States is an interesting example of the use of Zotero to generate e-reserve reading lists (Kimball, 2010). Amherst is a private college serving a student population of approximately 1700 undergraduates. They implemented Drupal as their CMS system in the autumn of 2009 after having switched from Blackboard. Within Drupal, their E-Reserve Builder includes an Import tab that allows instructors to upload a file of Zotero references. E-Reserve Builder also includes time-saving options such as *search e-reserves* so that faculty, TAs, or librarians can add readings already in Drupal to courses directly from their search results. Amherst's Drupal implementation is set up with sorting flexibility, so that students have the option of sorting their reading lists by author, type (PDF, Weblink), or due date.

The iTunes U approach

Relevance of iTunes U for libraries

Much has been written about the popularity of search engines like Google, and undergraduates' reluctance to select their library's subscribed databases as a preferred source for locating references (Gross & Latham, 2009; De Rosa, Cantrell, Hawk & Wilson, 2006). Recognizing students' self-assessment as self-sufficient or even expert searchers, and that search engines like Google Scholar provide access to scholarly content as well as more popular fare, librarians are acutely aware of the need for vigilance in ensuring continued relevance of libraries to their student populations.

Apple's iPod is immensely popular with today's college and university students. Looking around any North American campus, one is inclined to agree with Apple's assertion that '[iPod and iTunes] is a familiar and essential part of their lives' (Apple Inc., 2009). This assertion is supported by the fact that as of 2007, Apple had sold over 100 million iPods (Neumayr & Monaghn, 2007). Because many students are familiar with iTunes, using it to update content on their iPods, iTunes U affords libraries, as well as the larger institution to which they belong, an opportunity to improve student success and to build more positive perceptions of library relevance. Inclusion of library resources, services, or content within an institutional iTunes U site enriches technology already popular with the user population by embedding library resources.

History and overview of iTunes U

iTunes U was developed with early pilot partners including Duke and Stanford universities beginning in the mid-2000s. After the pilot phase was completed, iTunes U was launched more widely to Canadian and American institutions in May 2007, and in June 2008 Apple extended its reach to include institutions outside of the U.S. and Canada (Ashling, 2008). Now, institutions from Australia, Austria, Belgium, Denmark, Finland, France, Germany, Ireland, Italy, the Netherlands, New Zealand, Norway, Spain, Sweden, Switzerland, and the United Kingdom are eligible to apply for an iTunes U site. As of August 2009, 100 colleges and universities had public iTunes U sites live within the Apple store, and over 200,000 educational files were available (Apple Inc., 2010). Many of these institutions also have an internal site restricted to faculty, staff, and students, and some additional schools offer only an internal site.

The iTunes software, available for free download, was designed originally as a distribution channel for purchasing and downloading music to the iPod. Users can also utilize iTunes to upload their CD collections to their iTunes music library, and can then download library tracks to their iPods. The iTunes store can be accessed from a left hand side menu within the iTunes software. The iTunes store is a marketplace for purchasing songs, albums, and other content that, once purchased, is added to the user's library and can be downloaded to the iPod. More recently, as new generations of iPods began to include video screens with full color display and with the release of Apple TV, the iTunes store's offerings expanded to include video content such as music videos, movies, and television programs for users to purchase or rent. It is within this iTunes store marketplace that iTunes U has become available. A search for 'orbital' within the iTunes store now not only brings back content for sale by the electronic genre musical artist, but also retrieves lectures from

MIT's Principles of Chemical Science classes. A visit to iTunes U within the iTunes store illustrates that college and university sites co-exist for public, free consumption alongside offerings from museums, art galleries, educational television providers, and others. The public iTunes U site accessible from within iTunes allows these organizations to market themselves to a broad audience as a recruitment, marketing, or public relations tool. Some institutions like Stanford in the U.S. and the U.K.'s Open University, whose mission includes the provision of education for the general public, also take advantage of the free iTunes U platform to deliver educational materials to the public. It has also been recognized as a way to offer content to alumni, a group that is often not well served in terms of electronic library collections. Content available from academic institutions includes audio and video recordings of lectures, interviews, promotional videos, podcasts, video tutorials, and more.

iTunes U as a course management tool and e-reserve

Benefits

iTunes U is a very attractive option for academic libraries because it is free and because it offers a way to add the university and library content within a platform that users already frequent. Apple's administrator guide for iTunes U describes iTunes U as follows:

> Based on the same easy-to-use technology as the iTunes Store, iTunes U features Apple simplicity and portability and is designed as a service for institutions to manage a broad range of audio, video, and PDF content, and to make it available quickly and easily to students, instructors, staff, alumni, and, optionally, the public. (Apple Inc., 2008)

Apple's education site promotes iTunes U as a way for the academic institution to support today's students' digital lifestyle (Apple Inc., 2009). The iTunes U content can be set up for download to the iPod or iPhone (except the PDF content) or for viewing on the students' computer. Since the iTunes software can be downloaded for a Mac or a PC for free, it is accessible to all students provided they have a computer and Internet access. Mobile device support is also a current trend in library literature, and implementing iTunes U is one option for fulfilling this.

Because iTunes was designed for music content and has been developed to now distribute video content as well, iTunes U is a natural fit for instructional audio and video content. iTunes U has been utilized by libraries as a platform for delivering library tours, instructional videos, and promotional videos. For an overview of one such project, see a recent article reporting the vodcasting experience at Miami University in Ohio, USA (Michel, Hurst & Revelle 2009). iTunes U is also a natural fit for delivering class lectures. In terms of course readings, there is potential for utilizing iTunes U for e-reserve, as URLs can be added within the links area of a course, and PDFs can be added as *tracks* for a course.

Limitations

iTunes U appears to be currently utilized primarily for the audio and video formats. The authors hypothesize that this is because these are the formats for which iTunes U was designed. PDF format is generally used to deliver PDF versions of PowerPoint lecture slides, or transcripts of accompanying audio visual content. Also, the metadata fields available to describe uploaded content are appropriate for music or video files, but not for books and journal articles. For example, there is an album field, but only one title field, so an article title and journal title would have to be slotted in to separate fields that are not necessarily appropriate. The links area is a possibility for adding e-reserve readings, but is unstructured, and there are likely character and display limits. Institutions utilizing iTunes U generally have a CMS that they use for course readings and other course content, linking out from the CMS to supplementary content on iTunes U. Duke and Stanford Universities, two of the early iTunes U pilot projects, are examples of this. Duke utilizes Blackboard and the iTunes U building block to log students in automatically from Blackboard to iTunes U, and Stanford uses Sakai with integrations for iTunes U.

Authentication and institutional content

While there is a wealth of materials available for public viewing and download, institutions participating in iTunes U can also create an internal iTunes U site, either as their only iTunes U presence, or as a sub-section of a public site restricted to current students, faculty and staff. iTunes U supports shibboleth and other authentication methods via a transfer script. This means that regardless of your local authentication method, your system can talk to Apple's so that users are authenticated without an additional login. Authentication for access and other permissions is accomplished by establishing what Apple refers to as user credentials. Credentials can be defined at both broad and narrow levels. For example, a generic student or faculty member can have defined credentials that allow them appropriate access to content on your iTunes U internal site, and Jane Doe, a first year student enrolled in Psychology 101, can have credentials allowing her to download lectures from her class, but not from classes in which she is not enrolled. On the content side, audio, video, and PDF files can be uploaded to course pages. Content uploaded to course pages appears within the iTunes U display area. It is organized into groups which are displayed as horizontal tabs below the basic course information. Groups can be defined in terms of content type, with one tab for audio, another for video and a third for PDF transcripts, or using another organization scheme like lectures, interviews, and reading materials. Groups can be associated with a user's credentials to allow or restrict access to specific content or to specific activities that can be accomplished with that content. For example, iTunes U includes a drop box group type for students to upload assignments. Depending on the nature of the course, the instructor or iTunes administrator can define user credentials so that students cannot view one another's work, but can upload and view their own. Similarly download, view, and edit/administer can be defined at the individual user or content group level and can vary within a course. Because there can be up to 100 credentials per user, this process of assigning credentials has the benefit of flexibility for complex courses and institutions, but can also be a time-consuming and daunting task. Fairfield University's implementation of their iTunes pilot project illustrates this, as they reported having to get assistance from Apple professionals to help them to achieve a seamless login process for students. Full integration of the student login process with their local authentication system was a big issue for them (Potocki, 2006).

Adding content to iTunes U

As mentioned above, iTunes U supports multiple file types, and also allows the creation of links. When they implement iTunes U, institutions can choose whether they want to upload content to the iTunes U server or if they want to use their own server space. If they choose to upload to Apple, then the process is very simple. This is done via a Web-based form. Once authorized to do so, an instructor can add files to their courses by clicking on an edit link from the course page. The Web form indicates a default tab, or location for the file, which can be changed by selecting an alternate tab. The instructor then uses a browse button to locate the file on their computer. This process is very similar to attaching a file to an email message, but can take some time as audio and video files tend to be large. Uploaded files appear as tracks in the tab chosen for display within the course page.

Integration of iTunes U and CMS/LMS

Several American Universities have implemented iTunes U. In 2009, a Blackboard iTunes U extension that Vanderbilt University created in partnership with Apple and Blackboard was made available for download on the Blackboard extension site (Blackboard Inc., 1997–2010). The extension is compatible with Blackboard version 8 and higher. Once installed, the iTunes U extension makes the process of setting up links to iTunes U courses from Blackboard simple for instructors. The extension presents itself to instructors as an option within the Control Panel's course tools. The faculty member sees an iTunes U option within that area. If the Blackboard and iTunes U administrators at the institution have enabled content for that professor's login, then he or she can begin setting up content right away. If there is nothing set up, then a notice invites the instructor to request access from the administrator. Once an iTunes U course is set up, it is linked with that instructor's Blackboard account so that when he or she chooses the iTunes U course tool, he or she can choose to add an iTunes U link as a specific content type that is automatically linked to his or her course on iTunes U. By default the link is to the course level. It is also possible to create links to the course with a particular file pre-selected, but this requires copying the iTunes store URL from iTunes and pasting it into Blackboard. For an excellent demonstration of both faculty set-up instructions and student access, refer to the Spring Arbor University's Office of Academic Technology's YouTube tutorials for faculty members (*http://www.youtube.com/watch?v=dV_ALYK_x_o*).

As of August 2009, the authors could not locate an institution utilizing iTunes U for e-reserves. Both Stanford and Duke universities, who were pilot partners with Apple, utilize a course management system for the e-reserves portion of courses and utilize iTunes U for audio visual content. Duke utilizes Blackboard and the library catalogue as the access points for e-reserves, and Stanford uses an implementation of Sakai. Both of these CMSs talk to iTunes U, but it does not appear as though required readings are there.

Notes

1. Though somewhat out-of-date, a comparison of select citation management software is available on Wikipedia at: *http://en.wikipedia.org/wiki/Comparison_of_reference_management_software*
2. The quality of the metadata varies depending on the indexing service used to populate the CM software. Sources like Google Scholar may not include complete bibliographic details. Sources may contain errors due to data entry mistakes that are then repeated by the CM software output.

5

New digital media formats

Streamed video

Brief description of technology

Streaming media can be defined as Webcasting with on-demand delivery, where the user pulls down the content, often interactively. Streamed media is delivered direct from the source (the server) to the client (the media player) in real-time. This is a continuous process, with no intermediate storage of the media clip on the client machine. More specifically, streaming media is digitally encoded files delivered over the World Wide Web or IP (Internet Protocol) broadcasting (Austerberry, 2005).

Streaming technology allows multimedia servers to deliver content in a continuous stream that can be decoded and played back within seconds after being received, while in contrast, the process of downloading even a short video clip may take several minutes. Streamed presentation is thus timesaving, even on a 28.8 modem (Song, Nixon, & Burmood, 2001).

The fact that files are only viewed, but not stored by the user, has important implications for libraries and copyright. The library, and by extension the copyright holder, remains in control of the content as it cannot be illegally saved or rebroadcast. No peer-to-peer distribution or file-sharing is possible.

Advantages over traditional video

The merits of streamed video for supporting distributed learning are obvious – simultaneous instant remote access 24/7, no need for distribution or duplication of physical items, no problems with damaged media formats needing to be replaced, and less physical space required for storage of programs. Research has found 'that students prefer to access educational videos on-line rather than using physical library facilities' [due to] 'ease of access, flexibility, and students' control over study time, space, and learning materials' (Chen & Choi, 2005: 475).

Streamed video in electronic reserve

Survey, Web conference, and Web search results

In December 2008, the authors surveyed American, Canadian and some Australian university libraries on their e-reserve practices, and followed the survey with a Web conference, inviting participation from college and university libraries in Ontario, Canada, who share an interest in the subject. The survey of e-reserve indicated that nearly 25% of the libraries were offering links to in-house streamed video, and about 20% links to video streaming databases. The Web conference and a Google search revealed additional university libraries that are offering streamed video in electronic reserve. At the libraries where streamed videos are delivered through e-reserves, practices varied, but there were some commonalities. Just as with other media in e-reserves, the most common means of linking to streamed video, for both in-house streamed content and video databases, was through commercial course management systems. The next most popular method was through proprietary or open source e-reserve software, followed by the use of an integrated library system OPAC, and through commercial and open source digital repository software. The issues related to using these methods for streamed video are much the same as they are for other media.

Within the Province of Ontario, one institution has been offering two nursing series of 50 videos to 700 distance students, cost-sharing with the Nursing School, using the Bibliocentre's Video on Demand (VoD) streaming service. The Bibliocentre, a division of Centennial College in Ontario, Canada has acted as a cooperative on behalf of the Ontario Colleges of Applied Arts and Technology. In addition to offering curriculum-related streamed video for the past few years, they have also been providing automatic super indexing/annotating or metadata and video clips or *learning objects* for enhanced access to video resources. The fate of this video project is now in some doubt as the Bibliocentre was closed down in mid-2009, due to funding problems, and has been replaced by the Ontario College Library Service (OCLS), which will continue some, but not all, of the Bibliocentre's services. Another Ontario provincial video streaming initiative, currently in the planning stages, is Video Ontario, a project under the auspices of Knowledge Ontario, supported by the Government of Ontario, the Ontario Council of University Libraries, and the Ontario Library Association. Another university library has purchased its own Media Streaming Server, and the Library IT staff convert in-house instructor videos for streaming. Others create links to videos streamed by IT departments. Streaming formats used include AVI, RealVideo, Apple QuickTime, Adobe Flash, MPEG, MPEG-4, WMV (Windows Media Video) and are viewed using the appropriate players, e.g. RealPlayer, QuickTime Player, Windows Media Player.

An interesting development of the e-reserve survey and subsequent Web conference was a burgeoning of interest in communication and sharing of information on e-reserve among Ontario academic libraries, which led to University of Guelph-Humber hosting an e-reserve seminar in June 2009.

Academic literature review

Although Web searches, the survey and the teleconference revealed that many academic libraries are offering streamed videos through e-reserve, very little has been written in the academic literature about this service.

Shephard (2003) used case studies to describe how streaming video is used, particularly in the United Kingdom, at the university level. He began with a literature review of the use of video to support student learning, beginning in the mid-1980s. He continued with a brief description of streaming video and how it differs from other forms of video, noting that streamed video retains more power in the hands of the copyright holders, as the video is never actually stored on the user's computer. He suggested ways in which streamed video could be used for pedagogical purposes, then analyzed a few specific case studies of universities' use, all of which took place during actual lectures to support on-campus learning, with no involvement by the libraries.

Thomas (2004), of the Clemens Library at the University of Virginia in the United States, provided information on a wide variety of streamed video content then available freely on the Web, and discussed the digitization of rare primary source film and video footage from their own university, done by their Robertson Media Center. While this is not an e-reserve style project, the library was involved in video streaming through their Digital Media Lab and created a Digital Library Production

Service, which is charged with creating and managing Web-deliverable video content. They tried whenever possible to adopt standard, non-proprietary output formats, firmly believing that open standards should prevail in the digital world. Thomas discussed the challenges of creating metadata for audio visual materials, and some of the research into technical aspects of searching. They linked to the digital through MARC records in the OPAC, as well as through a home-grown product, the Audio and Video Archive Tool, to manage both technical and descriptive metadata. Written in the early stages of video streaming in libraries, Thomas concluded that it was a bumpy ride, requiring constant adaptations, but worth the trip.

Eng and Hernandez (2006) described a situation at the Borough of Manhattan Community College in New York, in which streamed videos were developed as a part of electronic reserve, but they concentrated on the changing role of technical services and how taking on the management of video streaming invigorated the department. They originally turned to streamed video to create digital archival copies of high use videos in their collection. It is interesting to note that according to United States Copyright Law, they were within their rights to create archival copies of VHS recordings. In Canada, it is illegal to do this if a commercial copy of the title is available in another readable format. They also discussed the U.S. TEACH Act, which permits a much more liberal use of copyright materials for distance education than is allowed in Canada, so that they were able to stream and deliver video content without the cost and time constraints of requesting permission to copy. The library took on the technical aspects of the streaming, then added the links on password-protected course pages, and students were required to agree to a copyright statement before they could access materials. They went on-line in 2004, and they planned to institute a formal student feedback survey. Their experience has shown that 'embarking on a streaming video project may be as simple as extending an existing electronic reserves system to include another medium … it now makes little difference if the reserve material is a … film, a Word document, a PDF file or PowerPoint presentation, since an efficient work procedure with effective communication has already been established' (Thomas, 2004: 222). The Ryerson Library experience concurs with this.

In a very informative article, Prosser (2006) described a video streaming project at Northern Lakes College in the Province of Alberta in Canada in 2005/6. Although the term e-reserves is not used, the situation is similar, as the streaming was done by the library for course-specific delivery. The reasons for embarking on the streaming initiative and the issues involved in its implementation and delivery strike a universal chord. First, there were the geographical barriers, as they have thirty sites scattered over a service area in Alberta of over 165,000 square kilometers. These sites or trailers are very small in order to be transportable, so there is little or no physical storage capacity on site. Physical delivery methods or library-to-site loans of VHS and DVD copies were found to be costly and inefficient. Secondly, there were the time constraints – teachers asking for the same resources at the same time in the curriculum. Then there was the competition. With a vigorous climate of online education in Alberta, they felt the need to keep up with new resource delivery technologies capable of engaging students and enriching classes. The timing was right. In the past, smaller institutions in Alberta did not have the technological means or sufficient money to build their own LANs (local area networks) or WANs (wide area networks). The creation of the Alberta SuperNet, a high-speed, high-capacity broadband network linking government offices, schools, health-care facilities and libraries, funded by the Alberta Government, enabled the college with enough bandwidth to start streaming videos over the Internet.

MonD software was selected by Northern Lakes College (NLC) library for streaming because of its flexibility and the fact that it allowed the addition of material from any vendor by using the MonD Manager. As a result, they were not restricted to content from a single vendor, and in addition, they were able to reconfigure the video content already owned from VHS to video streaming format, provided they could obtain licensing agreements from the producer. The software allows indexing and the insertion of keywords, but the library was reliant on these being made available from the video producers, which was not always the case, so not all titles are indexed. Furthermore, they do not have catalogued records of available videos within the OPAC (Sirsi/Dynix) with URLs pointing the student to the actual videos.

It is important to note that Northern Lakes College owns the digital content. Stability and reliability of content are important in an educational setting. If video content is dependable from year to year, then teachers are more likely and better able to include the material in their curriculum. Another advantage of the software is that it is possible to track title use. Reports may include usage statistics for individual, selected, or a comprehensive list of video titles. NLC's video streaming project will be evaluated on the basis of student and staff use. There is however a technical limitation to the system. They cannot use the videos with ease within the WebCT and Centra course management software used by NLC. Video streamed material has to be reconfigured to work within either of these systems and even then only clips of entire videos may be used. Part of the issue is bandwidth usage: although SuperNet has increased capacity tremendously, they are still not able to stream these very large video files comfortably within the course management systems.

Prosser continued by stressing the importance of encouraging the participation of teaching staff in selecting video streaming content as it increases the initial sense of participation and buy-in to library services, but she noted that a great deal of time was needed to explain to teachers what video streaming entailed and how it could be used. Another challenge is the lack of standardization among vendors, with different technology, different delivery methods, different content, different pricing, different license agreements, and different indexing offered. Some of the material can be owned, some can be leased for one or more years. She noted that librarians are familiar with these kinds of complications, but at the moment it seems to be a particularly intricate process to secure video streaming content. (This is borne out in the report on the Digital Delivery Discussion Group below, and by the Ryerson Library experience, discussed in the case study following.)

For the Northern Lakes College library, branding is a big challenge. The MonD Player desktop icon sits on the desktops of staff and students, and librarians are puzzling over how to bring it into the library field so that students and staff recognize this as a library service as opposed to an IT service or even a free Internet service. This is important insofar as results of exit surveys are tied to funding and provision of services, so it is important to impress upon the user that these materials are bought and presented by the library.

In 2007, Brown University Library in Rhode Island added video and streaming video to its Online Course Reserves Access system, linking faculty-selected titles for specific courses through their campus course management software ('Add Video', 2007). The library Website notes that full-length movies, short video clips, and audio files can all be placed on Reserves. Links to reserves in all formats is through the MyCourses site.

Gibbs (2009) described a library streaming project at Coventry University in England. As with Prosser, the term e-reserve is not used, but the videos are course specific and have been linked through the OPAC, the university's VLE (Virtual Learning Environment) software, and the Equella, digital repository software. The copyright situation in the United Kingdom is somewhat different from other areas, as the use of off-air recorded audio visual material is regulated by the Educational Recording Authority, enabling licensed academic institutions to record broadcast materials for non-commercial use in education and research. It is this kind of off-air material that Coventry streamed, therefore they did not have to negotiate with video distributors for rights to stream and pay the costs. Their library has a large and active video collection used in class presentations. Their consideration of streaming began when they were in the transition from VHS to DVD, which gave them the cue to review their video service and devise new strategies for delivery. Then in 2007, the university formed an e-Learning Unit with the specific agenda of supporting the institutional VLE, which was to include e-learning tools and objects, and create an institutional repository. The streaming project was a collaborative effort by the library's Media Services, the university's IT services and the e-Learning Unit (ELU). Their reasons for streaming were as those listed previously under a previous section in this chapter on 'Advantages over traditional video'. They consulted with academic staff and were enthusiastically supported in launching a pilot project of four heavily used titles. Interestingly, she noted that demand for the service came primarily from health and business studies (as it is at Ryerson University Library discussed in the case study following).

The VHS tapes were transferred to DVD by Media Services, then streamed by IT. Gibbs provided details about the technical aspects of the streaming as well as protocols for naming and filing of programs. Initially, access to the streamed titles was available only on campus, through an 856 link in the library catalogue MARC record, direct to the item. Using persistent links from the OPAC, faculty were also able to put links to materials in course modules of the VLE. Users browsing the OPAC for digitized media items could do a keyword search for *streamed video* to bring up a full list of titles. Later, the ELU purchased Equella, a digital repository software, and the electronic link in the OPAC record was changed to connect to items through the digital repository, with access via a secure username and password, available over the Web, although links could be easily made back to the VLE software. The launch of the off-campus access led to an immediate and dramatic increase in use of the service. Gibbs concluded that their do-it-yourself approach has allowed them to test demand and tailor it to their needs, but that it is necessary to have good and on-going IT support, and that maintaining this IT support has been an issue for them.

Video-hosting Websites

There is also the potential for instructors and students to mount course-related video content on video-hosting Websites such as YouTube, and more dangerously, to add links to these sites on their Web pages without regard to copyright and licensing.

In her review article on YouTube culture and the academic library, Ariew (2008) noted that some instructors are using videos as primary source material to supplement class readings and to expand beyond the usual course devices. Students were asked to find YouTube videos that articulate ideas from required weekly readings. The students then posted their YouTube video links to Blackboard, sharing the videos along with other ideas in the class.

Ariew suggested that rather than competing with faculty, librarians can lead the way in helping their patrons find useful video sources. In order to be effective as video information specialists, librarians need to learn more about online videos: where they are hosted, how to find clips on various topics and subjects, how to evaluate the works, and how to discern which are most useful for those engaged in the teaching and learning process. Ariew then reviewed a number of Educational Video Hosting Sites which have been set up exclusively for educational or academic purposes, many of them sponsored by academic institutions.

> Research Channel, found at *www.researchchannel.org/* is sponsored by a consortium of research and academic institutions including the University of Michigan, University of Washington, and National Science Foundation. One finds presentations by scholars who share their work on research topics at a deeper level. This site includes a rich video library of 3,500 scholarly programs. (Ariew, 2008: 2059)

> Apple recently dedicated a free area in which higher education institutions can share content with students via the iTunes interface; iTunes U is billed as an application for 'the campus that never sleeps'. Also a link off the iTunes Store home page, iTunes U offers audio and visual content from a number of schools. The Massachusetts Institute of Technology makes some of its classes publicly available as part of its Open Courseware Project. University of South Florida Tampa Library, Arizona State University, and many others have extensive offerings of podcasts and videocasts providing instructional resources, promotional material, and special collections, oral histories, and archival material. iTunes U is a great way to reach patrons and to feature services and collections through video. (Ariew, 2008: 2058)

Dekker (2009) has also reviewed online academic video sites. Academic Earth, found at *www.academicearth.org*, features podcasts of lectures by professors from major American universities, which can be downloaded and shared, with a link to full citation information for the video. The Internet Archive: Moving Image Archive, found at *www.archive.org*, contains thousands of public domain films in a wide range of subject areas, including feature films. FORA.tv, found at *www.fora.tv*, offers video podcasts, mostly short lectures, debates, etc., from universities and research organizations, with much descriptive information. Film Archives Online, found at *filmarchives-online.eu* is a European database of educational films, with links to nearly 20 different film archives. Some films have been uploaded into YouTube for online viewing.

Critical issues: Pricing and rights management

In September 2008, a Digital Delivery Discussion Group was hosted by Gary Handman from the University of California in Berkeley in the United States, based on a White Paper, written by Handman and Lawrence Daressa from California Newsreel (a video distributor), at the National Media Market, held in Lexington, Kentucky. (The National Media Market promotes rich media to enhance learning by hosting a yearly one-stop selling and buying conference which educational digital and motion media buyers representing all types of institutions and agencies attend in order to preview and to make purchase decisions.)

This forum brought together selectors of educational media and representatives from the video distribution business, for an ongoing conversation about critical issues related to digital video access and distribution. Some members of the Ontario post-secondary audio visual sector attended and Cheryl Petrie, from the University of Waterloo in Ontario, Canada, reported the following. The university group identified serious concerns over pricing models for streamed content of educational titles (feature films were not under consideration) from distributors. Pricing that is based on FTE is unrealistically expensive and too volatile for budgeting projections. It is preferable to be given a pricing model up front, based on the cost of the program. Pricing and streaming contracts limited to single courses also put a similar burden on budgets. Streaming rights should be campus-wide (with password protection), as most titles are not specific to just one course, or even one subject, particularly with the trend towards interdisciplinary and multidisciplinary courses in universities. However, pricing practices to this date have made campus-wide access prohibitive. Obtaining pricing information takes too long, and there is too much back and forth between university staff and the distributors before a final price is reached (and Ryerson Library's experience confirms this). The pay-per-view model that has been suggested by some vendors was considered a poor idea, as it was too unpredictable, could become very expensive and would be hard to manage. Streaming rights for longer than just a single semester or one year were desirable. Perpetual rights are preferable, but that is not always possible, as distributors' contracts with film-makers have expiry dates. Reasonable pricing for at least a five year term would be the next best option. University members also made the point that streaming a program on campus does not mean that it goes to an expanded audience. Those who need to see it for their courses will see it whether the content is streamed and delivered on-line or the hard copy is viewed at home or in library workstations. The audience is still the same and the pricing structure should reflect that.

The distributors also provided their point of view on pricing models, noting some reasons for difficulties and the variance in cost factors in obtaining streaming rights. For example, film music rights expire and are often too expensive to renew. With many older programs, the contracts made at the time of the productions did not foresee digital online demand. Streaming was not an issue and the physical formats had a shelf life. When the distributors try to renegotiate for streaming, they often cannot come to a financially viable agreement with the producers; they noted that some programs may never become available for streaming.

Case study: The Ryerson University Library experience

Reasons for streaming: heavy use and relevance of collection

Ryerson University Library in Toronto, Canada has a collection of over 6,500 videos. These videos are not just an extra, but are an integral part of the teaching/learning process for a number of departments, particularly the Schools of Nursing, Business and Image Arts. These materials are heavily used, both for class presentations and individual review. Faculty bookings of library videos for class presentations approach 2,000 items per year.

Reasons for streaming: multiple user demand

By 2004, with a large increase in the distance education courses offered by Ryerson, access to videos was becoming a problem. Nursing students, in particular, are a large community of off-campus users in a department which relies heavily on instructional videos. Ryerson's School of Nursing is the largest nursing program in Canada, and delivers its courses in 33 different geographic centers around the province. In the past, the Ryerson Library had purchased videos to be held in one remote location and, in another case, had sent out a set of library videos by mail to another, but these were not satisfactory long-term solutions. In addition, nursing videos, being heavily used, are often physically damaged, and are very expensive to replace.

Ryerson's Business School, the largest undergraduate business school in Canada, also has high enrollments for courses, and divides them into smaller sections with a number of different instructors. For on-campus use, both nursing and business faculty often want to have multiple class screenings of the same videos on the same days, causing frustration to faculty when items are not available for booking. Titles in these two subject areas are about the most expensive in the library collection, often running to $1,000 a video (in Canada, educational institutions must pay for public performance rights for any videos screened in class, which adds a large cost to the price), so purchasing multiple copies is a costly answer to satisfying that demand.

Reasons for streaming: space

Space is another problem for the Ryerson Library. In 2007, the library exhausted its room for videos in the audio visual stacks, and had to shelve about half the collection in closed access, available on request only, with 48 hours notice, causing user inconvenience and extra staff time for retrieval. In 2008, room was found to move the collection to a larger area, but constant growth is already putting pressure on this space as well.

Reasons for streaming: technology

The latest external force which will affect the library considerably is that the university's Computer and Communications Services (CCS) is planning to remove VHS players from smart classrooms. The library collection is still predominantly VHS. DVDs are now being purchased as often as possible, but they do not have as long a life expectancy as VHS. They also get damaged much more easily than VHS, and often have to be replaced. As well, DVD technology is evolving, and may soon require adoption of new DVD formats, such as Blu-ray. In addition, it is likely that DVDs will be replaced by some other video medium in the not too distant future.

For obvious reasons, the library was anxious to go ahead with video streaming. However, the long road towards streamed videos, integration with E-Reserve and resulting cooperative projects with other related university departments has been a difficult one and full of set-backs.

History of Ryerson's streaming experience

External vendor/supplier

In February 2004, after discussions between the Audio Visual Librarian and a major Canadian educational video distributor which had a streamed component to their inventory, several scenarios were developed, with reasonable pricing, for offering streamed videos accessible through the Ryerson Library OPAC. A major attraction of this service was that the library would not have to do the streaming, find server space at the university, or request copyright permission to stream. The Audio Visual Librarian was very excited about this potential development, but, as is the case at most universities, there was a silo to break through. The hopes for offering streamed video were dashed when the university's CCS indicated that there would not be enough bandwidth for the library to proceed with this venture. The idea had to be put on the backburner for the time being.

In-house streaming

In November 2004, the library was approached by one of the Distance Education (DE) Coordinators about digitizing and streaming a library video and mounting it on the university's Windows Media streaming server, to make it available through a course Web page. When the bandwidth issue was mentioned, DE said that this was not a problem for them, so the timing seemed auspicious to re-visit the potential to stream library videos.

However, as well as technical considerations like bandwidth, there were copyright implications with video streaming. As noted above, to comply with Canadian copyright laws, the library must purchase public performance rights (PPR) for any video to be screened in the classroom, but these rights do not cover permission for digitization, which must be requested in addition to PPR.

For this first request to digitize and stream a library video, the distributor was contacted for copyright permission. As the request was only to digitize one part of a series which the library held in VHS and 16mm formats, permission was given to do so at no cost if the library purchased another copy of the complete series in DVD. Distance Education subsequently handled all the technical aspects and was soon offering the streamed video through the Blackboard's Content System module. The students could simply click on the Content tab within their Blackboard course, then on E-Reserve, then on the video title, and the Windows Media Player opened with the streamed video. With this success, CCS was consulted about expanding the range of streamed videos, and in January 2005, the library and DE were given the go-ahead to proceed.

External vendor/supplier re-contacted

In February 2005, the Audio Visual Librarian organized a meeting with the streamed video company representative, with whom she had consulted the year before, with librarians, and staff from DE and DMP. About 2,000 titles from the company's large collection of educational videos had been digitized and indexed with descriptive information (metadata) for online delivery from their own server, with instantly accessible parts of programs (learning objects) digitally bookmarked. It was a definite plus for the library that this extensive and time-consuming cataloguing metadata would be provided, and of particular interest was the fact that the videos had stable URLs, so that they could be linked through the OPAC, Blackboard, or course Website.

A trial account was set up in March for all the players to experiment with, and the E-Reserve technician was able to successfully create a link to one of the streamed videos through Blackboard. A Nursing professor agreed to work with the library during the summer on a pilot project for one course to be delivered in the Fall term 2005. Once exams were over, in May, another meeting was set up with the company representative to determine how they could fulfill the subject content needs of that particular course with video. The company representative gave an impressive demonstration of their streamed video system, and it was hoped that progress would be made quickly with this project, but then disaster struck. The company went into receivership. With that project on hold indefinitely, the library had to change direction, and began to work with DE on in-house streaming.

Procedures developed

Over the next few months, the library received increasing requests from DE for permission to digitize and stream library-held videos, again linking them through Blackboard for courses in a range of subject areas. At this point the librarians began developing procedures for processing streaming requests. Streaming was also new territory for video distributors. Most did not yet have a pricing structure for digitization rights, and were operating on a case-by-case basis. Some refused outright to have their videos streamed. With others, discussions began on pricing for various models of access: in perpetuity (which is difficult because distributors often have only limited contracts for distribution, not perpetual rights themselves); for the whole university through the OPAC (authenticated through EZproxy as is done for the library licensed databases); for a limited time, such as one or two semesters; for a limited group, such as one class through the OPAC E-Reserve; or through the (course-specific password protected) Blackboard course management system.

Links within Blackboard, integration with E-Reserve

The restricted Blackboard model was preferred by most distributors, and for this reason, streamed video requests were integrated with E-Reserve, and requests for streamed videos were added to the on-line E-Reserve Request Form. Requests for library-held, or newly ordered library materials were initially processed through the Audio Visual acquisitions staff member. A form was developed for AV and E-Reserve to use for requesting digitization permission for both audio visuals to be streamed, as well as for text-based material to be scanned. The cost factor also had to be considered, and costs were monitored and approved by the Audio Visual Librarian, on a case-by-case basis. In 2005/6, about 15 library videos were streamed, at an average cost to the library of $250 each for streaming rights.

Staff issues and copyright

In order to keep track of library requests, at first a keyword-searchable note was added to the video item record in the library OPAC to the effect 'digital streaming rights requested as of [date]' and updating this with 'digital streaming rights obtained as of [date]'. But as requests increased, this proved to be an inefficient manual way of dealing with the information and was soon abandoned.

Distributors were asking for more information about the use of the streamed videos than publishers requested for scanning print material. The library AV acquisition staff member was merely acting as an intermediary between DE and the distributors during the process. He was spending valuable time passing messages back and forth between the two groups, and streaming requests were getting delayed. DE had all the relevant information about the courses: number of students, course duration, expected use of videos, etc., and in several cases DE instructors had already spoken directly to distributors about streaming rights and or obtaining specific titles. One Nursing professor successfully negotiated with the distributor and secured free streaming rights for DE for a popular ten part nursing series, held in the library. In some cases DE were streaming instructors' copies of videos not held by the library, or creating their own in-house video content (such as guest lectures, role-playing scenarios) to stream for specific courses. DE had the financial resources not only to hire their own copyright permissions staff person, but also to pay for the streaming rights for use for specific distance courses. It seemed that since rights were granted on a course rather than university-wide basis, the efficiency of having DE take on this work out-weighed the lack of library control over streaming rights. While the streaming request option on the E-Reserve form was retained, particularly for on-campus courses, it seemed that in the interest of speed and efficiency, the form might be by-passed in some cases and DE would go directly to the distributor and pay for rights from their own funds.

With video streaming added to the Reserve Request Form, requests for streamed content for campus classroom-based courses, as well as for Distance courses were received. As DE were only responsible for their own courses, the AV technician then worked with the Digital Media Projects Office, who did the streaming for on-campus courses, also linking to the video from Blackboard.

DE shared database concept

In December 2005, DE approached the E-Reserve unit about the idea of setting up a database to track the status of e-reserve requests that could be accessed by the library, DE staff and faculty making the requests. The concept was based on a previous database they had created for the

Ryerson Bookstore, which allows DE instructors to request book purchases, to monitor the departmental approval process and check for items received. The Bookstore, apparently, benefited from the ease of communication with faculty clients, and faculty were able to obtain the information they wanted when they wanted it. The rest of the Continuing Education (CE) Department, of which DE is a part, embraced the idea of a shared database with the Bookstore, and their faculty also requested participation.

Fast on the heels of success and keen on speeding up the processing of e-reserve requests in anticipation of increased demand, the DE Department offered to provide all necessary technical support to the E-Reserve/DE project. They would absorb the cost of programming, load the data on their server, and be responsible for future maintenance of the database. Unlike the Bookstore database, which was built from scratch, the E-Reserve/DE database would stem from the existing Microsoft Access-based files created by E-Reserve's Copyright Lead Hand, the staff member responsible for coordinating and tracking permission requests to publishers.

As this project involved a non-library partner, E-Reserve was careful to consult widely with the library's systems personnel, Audio Visual Services and Library Council, the librarians' group responsible for policy and administrative decisions. A small DE/E-Reserve working group was established in January 2006 to examine the data required to build the database. The group identified the appropriate field names, levels of access and required data for different user groups (faculty making e-reserve requests; library/DE staff looking up information; DE/E-Reserve/AV acquisition staff processing the requests). When completed, the faculty would be able to log into the database, input course reading requests and have the E-Reserve staff check them against the library holdings. If the request involved copyright clearance and/or scanning of documents, library staff would be able to check the progress and outcome of the requests at any time. This capability would allow staff to determine a new alternative for filling the request if necessary, such as print course packs, depending on the copyright cost and funding availability. Many hours of phone calls and emails would be saved by all parties concerned (faculty and DE/AV/E-Reserve staff) through this new tool. It was also hoped that this database would become a central location for digital rights permissions related to course readings, providing information on the requestor of permissions (faculty; DE; the library), the format (text; AV) and terms and conditions for permissions granted (gratis vs. cost; perpetual rights vs. specific durations, etc.). A different level of access would enable AV or E-Reserve staff to look up the contact information of rights owners and generate request letters for copyright clearance. Faculty, with their access permissions to the database, would not see such details but would obtain some idea of the amount of time and cost (if any) involved.

Collaboration on media library concept

Unfortunately, there was another set-back; this database became stalled due to work pressures in DE. However, DE decided to apply the same concepts and created a database for themselves to keep track of copyright permissions for videos they had streamed. At this time, the AV staff person was using a cumbersome Access file to track requests. After a meeting with library staff, DE considered allowing the library Audio Visual technician administrative access to the database, to use this platform instead of her Access file, and to add additional information. (For example, their database raised a red flag to indicate copyright permissions expiry dates, but the note said 'contact the library'.) With access to the database, the AV technician would be able to go in and add the copyright holders contact information. At this meeting, it came to light that DE did not know that DMP were also streaming videos for the library. The library arranged a subsequent meeting to include DMP staff, with the happy result that DE planned to cooperate with the library and DMP. So that efforts would not be duplicated, and all the information would be available in one place, it was suggested that DMP could also use the DE database to keep track of permissions for videos which DMP had streamed.

Demand for streamed content continues to increase with the growing enrollment in distributed learning courses at Ryerson. It is essential to keep the channels of communication open to avoid any duplication of effort over streaming, as well as to insure that any streaming of library materials is done within copyright restrictions. The shared database project would help address concerns in managing these issues. This cooperative project is currently not yet functional, as DE have not had time to do the additional work on the database. An off-shoot of this cooperation led to the library initiating a first-ever meeting with all the video streaming players from a number of different departments throughout the university, which has subsequently led to additional cooperative pilot projects between the library and other groups.

Moving ahead

In April 2008, video streaming moved ahead in a major way, when a large nursing series of 64 videos was purchased along with streaming rights, streamed by DE and made accessible for specific courses through Blackboard. In the same year, a set of heavily-used fashion videos, developed by a Ryerson faculty member, were also successfully streamed, and made available through OPAC E-Reserve, considerably lessening pressure and waiting time for these popular videos. In the academic year 2008/9, an additional 30 library videos, at faculty request, were streamed through E-Reserve.

The library is increasingly trying to negotiate with distributors for streaming rights for the whole university, rather than individual courses, in hopes of achieving cost savings as well as increased access. More distributors have also jumped on the streaming bandwagon, and companies like Films for Sciences and the Humanities offer streamed content from their own server, accessible through both the OPAC and course management systems such as Blackboard. The National Film Board of Canada (NFB) has considerably increased access to online content, with their Online Screening Room of over 800 titles free for home use, and available to universities for an annual subscription of $899 for the whole university. Each film carries its own URL and can be embedded quite easily into other online media, emailed or shared on Twitter, Digg and del.icio.us. It also offers Described Video and Closed Captioning capabilities (Dekker, 2009). The stable URL facilitates the potential for linking in e-reserve. In October, 2009, NFB launched their iPhone application, downloadable free from iTunes, so that their library of on-line videos can be watched on the smart phones.

Ryerson Library has also subscribed to two major streamed video databases, *Theatre in Video* and *Dance in Video*. Both these databases allow faculty to create playlists. These databases have the capability for users to create playlists or folders (collections of tracks, albums, images, clips, reference material, and even other playlists) around a specific theme, so that materials selected or downloaded can be shared with/ viewed by other users. This presents opportunities for faculty to create reading lists to share with students in their classes, an equivalent of the e-reserve concept, but so far none have been through the library's E-Reserve department. In addition, the ProQuest Nursing database provides nearly 100 training videos which can be downloaded and included in reading lists.

Lessons learned

Over the course of several years, the Ryerson Library's journey towards streamed video has offered many valuable lessons. First, if streamed video is a priority, then a way can be found to make it a reality. Faced with roadblocks, the library continued to persevere until the goal was accomplished. Collaboration and partnerships are keys to success. Because of the convenience of streamed video, faculty and students will buy in to the idea, and they can be useful allies in looking for funding opportunities and/or applying pressure to secure funding. Libraries need to be proactive and look for other stakeholders at their universities, commercial vendors or even other institutions. Working with IT departments and distance education schools, and becoming involved in course management systems can create beneficial personal contacts, earn respect for the library and give the library clout to help achieve its objectives. Cost-sharing and/or staff-sharing with other departments should be investigated, while local and/or provincial, state-wide consortia should be considered. Libraries must show a willingness to adapt to new technology and experiment with different ways of delivering digital multimedia.

6

Challenges and issues

Copyright: How copyright impacts on e-reserve delivery and process

Library services have always been affected by copyright laws. Licenses are signed with copyright collectives and royalties are paid on the amount of photocopying done on campus machines. In some countries, such as Canada, desk-top delivery of interlibrary loan materials is not allowed and public performance rights are needed for classroom showings of media content. Access to electronic journal databases is limited to the local academic community, as subscription fees are normally based on current student enrollments of individual institutions. E-reserve by far is most impacted by copyright permission cost and the service is dependent on responses from rights owners to approve online postings of materials. The copyright-seeking process and record keeping are labor-intensive and e-reserve staff are directly involved in interaction with faculty to decide on what course materials can be legally included for online delivery. Copyright laws may vary across countries but the impact on the e-reserve process is a common issue.

To ensure that teachers and students carry out personal research and teaching activity without fear of infringing copyright, libraries must engage in a balancing act of interests. Academic libraries in Canada have to comply with the Copyright Act, and in other countries, libraries must adhere to their specific copyright legislation. To protect authors and content owners, libraries must also be aware of restrictions as stipulated in licenses or contracts signed with content providers (as contract law takes precedence over copyright law) or copyright collectives acting on behalf of rights holders. At the same time, libraries must be knowledgeable about users' rights to access information in order to avoid unnecessary restrictions on faculty and student use.

What materials do not require copyright permissions from individual rights holders?

Photocopying

In the case of traditional print reserve services, there are various instances whereby academic institutions do not have to seek copyright permissions from individual rights owners before making copies of their works:

Materials in the public domain

Public domain is a copyright term that refers to work that belongs to the public. These could be works whose copyright protection has expired, usually 50 years (Canada) or 70 years (U.S. and Europe) after the death of the author. The copyright owner may also have stated that the copyright in his or her work is given to the public.

Exceptions in the Copyright Act

These exceptions permit educational institutions to copy parts of a copyrighted work unless the part is significant or valuable. The court will make the final determination of what is fair. Fair use (United States) and fair dealing (Canada) will be discussed in a subsequent section.

Licenses signed with copyright collectives

Copyright collectives are organizations that represent the collective interests of individual publishers or rights holders. Licenses and agreements are signed on behalf of their members with institutions so that these institutions do not have to approach individual publishers for permission to use their materials. The U.S. Copyright Collective is called the Copyright Clearance Center (CCC) and the Canadian counterpart is Access Copyright (formerly Cancopy).

Digital copying

In the case of e-reserve, there are instances whereby academic institutions do not have to seek copyright permissions from individual rights owners before making copies accessible online to users.

- If the institutions or faculty or students are the authors of the materials (such as lecture notes, exams, theses), e-reserve does not have to go beyond the institutions to seek approval for digitizing the materials.

- If faculty are using library subscription-based materials, such as journal articles from full-text databases, the licenses signed by the institutions with the database vendors cover online access by members of the community.

- Materials in the public domain and Exceptions in the Copyright Act (see under previous section on 'Photocopying').

How to determine what requires copyright permissions

Copyright legislation and fair use or fair dealing exceptions

Copyright complications are compounded in the digital age as copyright laws, like the Copyright Act in Canada, do not evolve fast enough to reflect the pace of technology. Libraries are caught in the middle of confusion in the interpretation of copyright legislation which, in some instance, is not appropriate for today's content, creation and delivery media. Most confusing is the proper application of the fair use or fair dealing exceptions in the copyright acts.

The fair use and fair dealing concepts share a common principle, but the U.S. fair use application is broader, especially in the educational context. For the purpose of teaching, it is not an infringement of U.S. copyright to make multiple electronic copies of portions of works for classroom use or to distribute them as online course materials. U.S. libraries generally claim fair use for the first semester's use and seek permission for re-use of the same materials for the same class in subsequent semesters. The item is removed at the end of each semester. The institutions' interpretation and application of fair use are often vetted by their local legal offices or Chief Information Officers. There is a lot of information on fair use in relation to e-reserve operations such as the University of Texas System site, developed by Georgia Harper; the Northwestern University site, *Copyright and the Electronic Reserve System*; the University of Washington site targeting faculty as its audience; and the American Library Association's address on fair use on its Web page (Burich & Rholes, 2004).

Nevertheless, even though the U.S. fair use application is broader and more flexible than the Canadian fair dealing, any use beyond the provisions allowed for in the Copyright Act still requires permissions from the rights holder(s) or from the copyright collective that represents the rights holder(s). What determines fair use is governed by four factors: the purpose of use, the nature of the work, the amount being used and the effect on market sales. The last factor is an important consideration, as students' access to posted online materials will influence their decisions to purchase a book or a journal, and faculty's repeated use of the same materials for courses (instead of new readings each time), may also affect market sales.

Canadian fair dealing provides exceptions for research, private study, criticism, review and news reporting but does not offer similar provisions for teaching and other educational purposes. The exceptions permit reprographic reproduction of published articles. Only a single copy can be given to a user. Delivery of interlibrary loan materials is limited. The copy that reaches an end-user has to be a print copy and any digital copy transmitted between libraries has to be destroyed.

The Canadian government is in the process of updating the Copyright Act. The Association of Universities and Colleges of Canada (AUCC), representing 94 Canadian public and private not-for-profit universities and university-degree level colleges, has been lobbying the government on behalf of its members to amend the Copyright Act to permit using new information and communication technologies as a medium for delivering course curriculum, and to include fair dealing provision for the purpose of teaching (Wills, 2004). At a roundtable on copyright reform in 2009, Steve Wills, representing AUCC, urged the government to update the existing educational exceptions 'to facilitate technology-enhanced learning and distance education, including the delivery of lessons through the Internet' (Wills, 2009: 3). A student should be 'allowed to view a lesson live through the Internet or later through a recording' and an academic institution should be allowed to make a recorded lesson available to a student for copying 'onto a computer or other mobile device for personal study later'.

Meanwhile, most libraries in Canada are cautious in applying a broader interpretation of fair dealing to e-reserve operations. Seeking copyright permission is the usual procedure taken. An article on copyright and e-reserves in the United States pointed out that 'the safest and most conservative approach is to simply pay for the use of everything in the electronic system ... this pathway should not be chosen lightly for it is very difficult to return to fair use once the library has sought and paid for permissions for everything' (Melamut, Thibodeau, and Albright, 2000: 23).

Recent lawsuits in the United States involving publishers and universities have raised questions about digital rights. Backed by the Association of American Publishers, Cambridge University Press and SAGE Publications have sued Georgia State University (GSU) for 'unauthorized distribution of copyrighted materials via its electronic course reserves service, its Blackboard/WebCT Vista electronic course management system, and its departmental web pages and hyperlinked online syllabi available on web sites and computer servers controlled by GSU' (Albanese, 2008: 16). Albanese reported that as of February 19, 2008, the suit charged GSU's e-reserve system with containing 'over 6700 total works available for some 600-plus courses'; making them 'available for electronic distribution'; and 'inviting students to download, view, and print materials without permission of the copyright holder'. The publishers were concerned that faculty and e-reserves provided extensive digital reading materials to students, such as multiple chapters of a book. Such a practice was perceived to be in violation of the fair use doctrine of copyright law and to affect market sales. The publishers were demanding that copyright permissions and licensing fees be paid to copyright owners.

As well as Georgia State, a number of other universities in the United States were also contacted by publishers about copyright infringements, resulting in stricter policies around digital licensing of materials (University of California, San Diego in 2003 and Cornell University in 2006). The GSU lawsuit is significant because it is the first case filed over e-reserve, and the publishers are academic publishers, not commercial ones. As Albanese (2008) observed, the case had serious implications for both the library circle as well as publishers. Albanese maintained that if the verdict favors the publishers, libraries would have to adopt a pay-per-use model for e-reserves. On the other hand, publishers may also find that they have forced the faculty to be more aggressively seeking other models for digital access, such as the university-based digital repository or open access.

The publishers' concern over copying in universities was not without precedent. In 1991, Basic Books and others sued Kinko, the printing, copying, and binding services company, for selling course packs of photocopied materials. In 1992, Princeton University Press and others sued Michigan Document Services for photocopying and producing course packs for University of Michigan students without seeking copyright permissions. To some observers, a parallel could be drawn between Georgia State's digital activities and those of Kinko and Michigan Document Services. Both were regarded as copyright infringement, although the GSU service did not involve monetary profit (Hafner, 2008). Carlson wrote about the legal battle over online reserves at the University of California and the interpretation of the fair use doctrine. Jonathan Franklin, Associate Law Librarian at the University of Washington and a fair-use scholar, was quoted as saying, 'institutions are so risk-averse that they license things they wouldn't normally have to license ... A legal battle might help clarify matters' (Carlson, 2005: A36).

License agreements

As well as interpreting exceptions in copyright legislation, e-reserve staff also have to deal with terms and agreements signed by colleges and universities with collectives that represent copyright owners or holders. The Access Copyright license held by universities and colleges in Canada is negotiated on their behalf by the Association of Universities and Colleges in Canada (AUCC). The fees are based on enrollment numbers of individual institutions, which cover the cost of permissions for photocopying done on campus machines falling outside the exceptions in the Canadian Copyright Act. This includes the copying of materials done for print reserve at the library. There is a specific limit to the amount of copying that can be done and an Exclusions List of publishers who are not represented by the license and therefore require separate permissions to copy. The Exclusions List spans several pages, including learned societies, scholarly and commercial publishers. There are separate fees for alternative formats (audio, Braille, large print for users who are visually challenged) microfiche, newspapers and out-of-print works. Under volume, no copying is to exceed 10% of a published work. The license authorizes one copy to be made per student, two for professors and also two for administrative purposes. The sale of copies is prohibited unless reported and paid for. The license does not cover:

- Crown publications (to be explained later);
- most print music;
- works intended to be used or replaced, such as workbooks;
- letters to the editors and advertisements in newspapers, magazines or periodicals;
- publications containing commercially valuable proprietary information, such as newsletters;

- works on the exclusions list; and
- works containing a notice expressly prohibiting photocopying under license with a reproductive rights organization.

The licenses signed with copyright collectives are not transferable to digital copying, as in the case of Access Copyright in Canada. The license specifically states that 'with the exception of digital transmission for the purposes of interlibrary loan permitted by this Agreement, nothing in this Agreement authorizes the dissemination or distribution of any Electronic File, in any electronic form in any way whatsoever ...'. For interlibrary loan, the digital transmission is limited to the transitional stage of faxing or electronic exchange through software such as Ariel transmission. The final copy that reaches the user must be in a print format. The Access Copyright license covers only copying done for the purpose of print reserve but does not provide for digital copying of print materials even in the library collection itself.

Crown copyright

The agreement signed by Canadian universities with Access Copyright does not cover Crown copyright. Crown copyright is a special form of copyright that exists in Commonwealth countries such as the United Kingdom, Canada, Australia, New Zealand, India and Kenya. It gives governments the rights to restrict reproduction or dissemination of information, subject to statutory exceptions. In a paper that discusses Crown copyright and the privatization of information, Colebatch (2008) demonstrates how these rights have created inconvenience for users as well as threatening to become a censorship tool for security and political reasons. To access government materials, the public has to rely on discretionary government licenses or limit their use to what is permitted under copyright legislation. Fair dealing exceptions are applied under certain circumstances, but copyright permission fees are normally required for reproduction and distribution of the entire work and commercial use of information.

In Canada and Australia, Crown copyright 'covers any work made by or under the direction or control of the government as well as any work published by or under its direction or control, so that simply publishing or directing the creation of a work automatically gives the government ownership of it' (Colebatch, 2008: 2). In contrast, the U.S. public can freely copy and distribute any government materials. Examples mentioned in the Colebatch paper included the report of the 9/11 Commission, published in various forms by different publishers, and images and videos from NASA 'used freely in books, documentaries, television programs, and even commercials', without the need to get permission or pay a copyright fee. However, even though there is no copyright for works produced by U.S. federal government employees, the state and local governments can still exercise copyright to prevent free access to certain information within their jurisdictions.

Developments in information technology have facilitated the wide dissemination of government information. They have also helped to spur public demand for free and immediate access. Colebatch (2008) described developments in the Commonwealth countries to limit the scope of Crown copyright and place materials in the public domain. She quoted such developments as in the United Kingdom in 1988, where the scope of Crown copyright was restricted to only works created by its employees during their service, and the elimination by New Zealand in 2001 of the Crown copyright in certain materials, which include bills, legislation, court decisions and commission reports. In 1997, Canada introduced 'blanket permission' for the reproduction of federal statutes and decisions of federal courts and tribunals as long as these uses meet accuracy and authenticity requirements. More recently, Natural Resources Canada made available to the public its topographic mapping data online, free of charge, for commercial as well as non-commercial use, provided that there is appropriate acknowledgement of the source of information made. Similarly, the Australian Bureau of Statistics (ABS) has in recent years 'made almost all of its statistics available online for free'. 'Some governments are exploring the use of Creative Commons licensing to free-up use of their materials.' Nevertheless, Colebatch (2008) concluded that a more comprehensive solution was needed for Crown copyright. Waivers and exceptions should not just apply to selective data. Ideally, Crown copyright should be 'formally waived', she said, and any retention for security or political reasons deemed as exceptions, rather than the rule.

How copyright impacts on e-reserve administration

Given the complexity of copyright legislation and confusion in interpretation in the digital environment, how do e-reserve operations in libraries respond to the copyright permission requirement? In Canada, the University of Windsor in Ontario conducted a library study in June

2004 (Dalton, 2007). Thirty-six post-secondary libraries in Canada were emailed with questions focused on copyright and e-reserve operations. Twenty-eight libraries responded. Eighty per cent replied that they had durable links to subscription-based online journals as the most frequent type of content; 70% included class notes provided by the professors, again materials that were copyright cleared; 65% included links to freely available Web pages; and 55% had links to class exams and course syllabi. All of the above did not require a copyright permission process, as these materials were subscription-based, or the authors (faculty or the institution) owned the rights, or they were in the public domain, whereby the authors released the rights to further distribution. Only 50% responded that they scanned copyrighted materials from print as part of e-reserve materials. As for the process itself, 60% preferred contacting the rights holders directly rather than seeking permissions through Access Copyright. Forty per cent of the respondents indicated that faculty members had to seek copyright permission themselves, and they appeared to use Access Copyright in most cases. The most frequent reasons libraries reported for not dealing with copyrighted materials were expensive cost, time-consuming process of seeking permissions and labor-intensive procedures. One respondent was quoted as saying the 'Canadian copyright law prevents us from mounting readings without prior permission and the costs of gaining those permissions, both actual and in terms of staff time (as experienced during our one-year pilot project) was exorbitant and unsustainable' (email from L. Carema, University of British Columbia).

A more recent questionnaire on the same subject was conducted by Ryerson University librarians in December 2008 (Appendix I). The fifty-seven respondents were mainly from North America and there were several Australian universities represented. Almost every e-reserve operation involved library staff doing the linking to electronic resources, with a small percentage (23%) done by faculty themselves. Seventy-eight per cent did not restrict the services to library-owned materials and provided links to external Websites or included university-authored lecture notes and tutorial solutions. Sixty-seven per cent of the respondents were involved in seeking copyright permissions and 71% were done by library staff, while 81% did not have an institutional copyright office. In many universities, the library was forced to take the leadership on copyright issues by default as other university departments did not want to have to deal with this difficult and complicated issue. Compared with the 2004 survey of Canadian universities previously described (Dalton, 2007), this extended survey of North American libraries and several

Australian institutions indicates an increased percentage in libraries' involvement in scanning documents and the copyright permission process.

Although copyright law is not the same in every country, there is little doubt that copyright compliance impacts e-reserve operations and management almost everywhere. In January 2003, all Council of Australian University Librarians (CAUL) were invited to participate in an information sharing exchange on their e-reserve management and operations. Twenty-five libraries responded in total. The report (Poleykett, 2003) indicated that the most significant event that advanced the development of electronic reserves in the country was the passing in 2000 of amendments (Digital Agenda) to the Australia Copyright Act of 1968. The amendments clarified what is legally required in making journal articles and book extracts available online, without seeking permissions from the copyright owners. Such copying for educational purposes is permitted as long as it stays within 10% of the whole limit. Institutions had to make sure that certain copying or communicating copies online would not exceed the statutory limits allowed by this legislation. Checking for copyright compliance became an important component of the e-reserve process. To accomplish that, 60% of the respondents chose to centralize the process of checking. Thirty-four per cent implemented a hybrid model where routine copyright issues were dealt with by staff in branch libraries and complex issues were referred to central staff that were more knowledgeable about copyright legislation. Most institutions seemed to see the importance of involving higher level staff in the task of copyright handling. Besides knowledge and understanding of the complex nature of Australian copyright law, a combination of tact, diplomacy, confidence and experience from library staff was required to liaise with faculty in cases of copyright infringement and refusal to mount materials online.

Despite the common recognition of the complex nature of copyright law, the survey in Australia (Poleykett, 2003) revealed that the majority of academic institutions in Australia did not have a centralized copyright office or officer to handle copyright matters. Forty per cent of CAUL respondents had a copyright coordinator or officer to manage copyright and provide advice for library related services. Some of the positions were wholly or partially funded by the university but located within the library. One respondent indicated the importance of the role of the officer in helping to promote faculty awareness of what materials are de facto copyright compliant (such as library subscribed databases) and what may be breaching the law (materials freely available on the Web).

In institutions with multiple libraries or multiple campuses, one way in which the digital culture has affected the organizational culture is that users are less tied down to local policies and procedures. They are only concerned with the speed of getting to the materials, wherever they reside. The University of Kansas Libraries in the United States implemented both decentralization and centralization in their e-reserve processing (Burich & Rholes, 2004). The digitizing workflow was decentralized and staff in each branch library converted print materials to electronic reserves. However, policies such as copyright and fair use interpretation had to be centralized to achieve consistency of application. As the CAUL survey revealed, there is no best practice or perfect model for e-reserve operations. A lot depends on the local situations, since e-reserve has to interact with services within and outside the libraries. 'Our initial conclusion that there were only three or four models in use around Australia was misleading, as significant variations existed with each model' (Poleykett, 2003: 8).

How copyright impacts on e-reserve workflow and process

Workflow issues

Schmidt (2002) discussed staffing issues for electronic reserves, comparing print or paper-based reserve with e-reserve in the number of steps involved in the operations. Schmidt listed twelve basic steps for print reserve:

1. Instructor submits materials for reserve.
2. Library processes materials for circulation.
3. Library processes copyright clearance.
4. Library files materials for access.
5. Library makes materials available for checkout.
6. Students request materials at desk.
7. Library retrieves materials.
8. Library checks materials out to student.
9. Student uses materials.
10. Student returns materials to desk.
11. Library files materials.
12. Repeat steps 6–11. (Schmidt, 2002: 24)

In comparison, Schimdt outlined the e-reserve workflow in four basic steps:

1. Instructor submits materials for reserve.
2. Library processes materials for scanning.
3. Library processes copyright clearance.
4. Library scans and mounts materials on server.

There was no need for steps 6–11 of the print reserve process, which involved filing, retrieving, checking in and checking out print materials. One can argue that some steps were missing in the e-reserve process, such as copyright review of faculty requests and creating electronic links to documents. These steps, especially checking faculty requests for copyright compliance, can be very time-consuming. In fact the biggest variable in the e-reserve workflow was the amount of preprocessing each institution chooses to do – whether library staff check each and every request submitted by faculty against library databases and evaluate sources to determine the application of fair use or fair dealing guidelines. In some cases, library staff will go back to the faculty to seek clarification for items that have incomplete information. To avoid risks of copyright infringement or to save time and labor in processing, some libraries limit copyright review to documents that do not involve complications, such as lecture notes, exam papers or links to library subscriptions.

When the University of Western Australia implemented the repository-based reading list management system, the migration of records from the library catalogue showed the impact of copyright on the organization of materials. Australian copyright law allows publishing online 'only one part of a literary work across the entire institution at any one time' (Poleykett & Benn, 2003: 7). Three chapters from a book copied would have to be combined into one file to be published online. While there were three bibliographic records in the previous system in the library catalogue, the repository allowed only one metadata record to be associated with each object. This legal requirement had the effect of reducing description to only the first chapter. Poleykett and Benn described how their staff had to manually review these records to decide on the best way to indicate the content of the file, such as whether to expand the descriptions to include all chapters of the file.

Another time-consuming component of the e-reserve process is record keeping. Schmidt (2002) outlined two parts in the process. The first is entering relevant bibliographic and course data into a database as materials are processed and scanned. Library staff identify materials that require permissions, which are cleared in most cases through CCC, while the rest are sent directly to individual rights holders. The second half is keeping track of charges and payment for copyright clearance. Even though the details may vary across countries due to differences in copyright legislation and copyright clearinghouses, the processes are just as complicated and labor-intensive where copyright is involved.

In response to the Ryerson University librarians' survey in December 2008 (Appendix I), 75% of the libraries indicated that they kept a separate database, mostly on Excel, to track copyright. Assuming such data is not automatically transferred into the database, the amount of staff time involved is substantial. To complicate matters further, copyright permission may not be readily available the first time library staff approach a rights holder. Library staff may be keeping note of first attempt, second attempt and subsequent efforts, referrals to other contacts, or eventual cancellations of requests due to all sorts of reasons such as excessive cost or exceeding deadlines for starting of courses.

Ryerson University Library was not an early starter in e-reserve, and had the advantage of learning from the experiences of pioneers. However, it does not appear that the complications in the e-reserve process have been resolved over the years and that the process has become less labor-intensive. When compared with the four basic steps as mentioned by Schmidt, Ryerson's workflow chart is like a maze (Figure 6.1). The extracted pages from Ryerson University's E-Reserve staff procedures in 2006 indicate the complexities of the process.

Copyright cost and payment issues

Electronic database subscriptions are usually based on the number of FTE at an institution and vendors normally advertise a set price for subscribers. Consortial purchases are effective in obtaining discounts. In contrast, copyright costs for e-reserve requests are totally unpredictable. First, e-reserve staff have no idea how many requests from a faculty member's list will require copyright permissions. Materials are checked against library subscriptions. If the library databases contain these articles, materials are already copyright compliant. If materials are in the public domain, there is no need to clear copyright. Secondly, publishers charge differently for copyright permissions. Academic publishers may grant approval for free, some publishers charge a flat fee while others use a formula based on number of students and number of pages. Payments invariably cover only a defined period such as duration of the course, academic term or a calendar year. It is difficult for e-reserve staff to know

Figure 6.1   Ryerson Library E-Reserve workflow

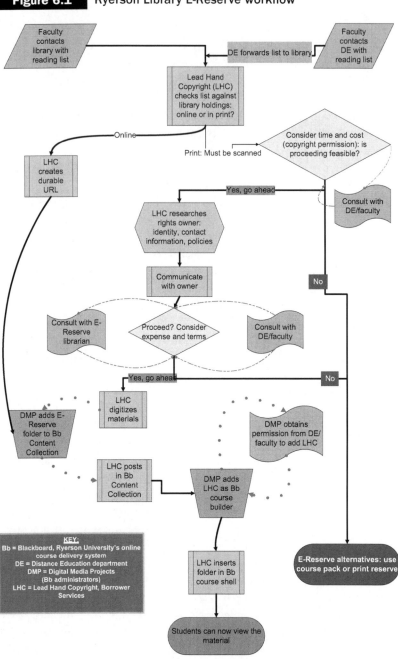

From Ryerson University Library, Toronto, Ontario, Canada. Used by permission.

ahead of time how much a document will cost until s/he contacts the publisher or rights holder and obtains a response.

The issue of copyright permission cost is one of the first things to be considered by librarians undertaking a pilot project of e-reserve. When Ryerson University Library started its e-reserve service in 2004, the librarian emailed other library colleagues in the Province of Ontario to find out their budgets and operational costs. In addition, she searched the library literature on this subject. Based on the information collected, an average amount was calculated to be used as an internal guideline for approving faculty requests. The criteria for approval include amounts per document, per course and per student. A large percentage of faculty requests were cancelled in the first year of operation, and one of the main reasons was copyright permission cost.

Bridgewater (2008) summarized the results of studies or discussions on e-reserve listservs on the average cost of a document. A pilot project was conducted at the University of Colorado in the United States in 2001 when an average of $35US per article or excerpt was considered a reasonable estimate at that time (Austin & Taylor, 2003). McGinnis (2000) reported an average figure of $29–40 US per article, based on her three-semester study at the University of North Carolina at Chapel Hill in the United States. In her own library at Washington State University in the United States, Bridgewater adopted a collaborative, phased approach. The library worked with one department on centralizing the copyright permission process within the library, set guidelines on payment options and consulted faculty in cases of excessive cost. The collaboration was eventually extended to the whole campus.

Who pays for the cost? Responses to an informal email survey conducted by Ryerson's E-Reserve Librarian in 2003 indicated that there was no uniform practice among Ontario libraries. One university library did not have limits on copyright spending. The service was so popular among faculty that it was hard to turn away requests. The librarian found it difficult to implement any generic guidelines, as the permissions for some subjects were known to cost more than others. Another library deliberately tested the waters with no limit on cost, only to discover that the cost escalated so high that they had to put a brake on spending and re-think the approval criteria.

Cubbage (2007) described the experience at Northwestern University in the United States, tracing the rising cost of copyright permissions, and the impact of turning down faculty requests to post documents on e-reserve due to cost. The U.S. fair use doctrine is not the same as Canadian fair dealing. Based on the fair-use principle, U.S. universities usually allow for 10% of a book or one article from a journal issue not available through an electronic subscription, to be scanned and posted electronically. Use is for one-time only. Requests for over 10% or repeated use will require copyright clearance. They saw the need for cost guidelines and put in a cost of $1 per page in 1998, absorbed by the library. In 2002/3, copyright cost rose to an average of $45US per item, so more than half of the requests were not processed due to high costs. The cost guideline was revised to $2US per page and up to $200US per item in 2003/4, but the costs continued to rise in 2004/5. Staff notified faculty of these copyright charges, which the library could not afford to pay and no academic department was willing to settle the payment from their own budgets.

An online discussion among academic librarians in Ontario, Canada took place in February 2009. At University of Guelph-Humber, the copyright permission cost was passed on to departments, especially those who could afford it and were keen on having the materials online. Most faculty, however, were reluctant to pay. The University of Guelph maintained their no-limit policy but cost was a prime consideration for acquiring the Atlas' Ares system to provide better statistics on use in relation to cost. Some keen interest was expressed among participants at the meeting to pursue a more liberal interpretation of fair dealing rights. The University of Calgary in the Province of Alberta, Canada, was cited as an example of a library justifying digitization practice as fair dealing in an educational setting. Most libraries, however, were not aggressive or proactive enough to push the envelope further. Seeking copyright permissions for materials, even when libraries had the print copies, appeared to be the norm, rather than the exception.

Copyright contacts issues

Seeking copyright permission is a time-consuming process. E-reserve staff often have to contact individual rights owners or holders (mostly publishers) and await their responses, which are unpredictable. Identifying the rights holders poses challenges, as there are times when e-reserve staff are referred from one source to another and from the publisher to the author. Getting in touch with the author is a daunting task, when the information is scant. Sometimes, it may not be easy to establish that a work is in the public domain.

The relative convenience of dealing with a copyright collective that represents individual rights owners is not always applicable in the e-reserve copyright seeking process. An article reported on the extent U.S. universities relied on the CCC for permission clearances, and revealed the following: in Austin's and Taylor's pilot study, 20 out of 75 articles used went through the CCC. In another instance, McGinnis attempted to contact the publishers directly but was referred to the CCC less than 10% of the time (Bridgewater, 2008).

Copyright tracking and statistics issues

Keeping track of copyright statistics is time consuming, especially if a library does not have a system customized for the purpose. Ryerson University librarians conducted an online survey in December 2008 (Appendix I). Of the 57 institutions that answered the question on keeping track of copyright requests, only 35% had commercial systems such as Docutek ERes whereas the rest of the institutions relied on separate databases, mostly on Excel spreadsheets. The next highly-used method was manual files, folders and cabinets. Only a handful reported that their institutions have developed home-grown systems to manage the data.

Ryerson Library realizes the problems associated with an inadequate copyright tracking mechanism. For a small pilot project in 2004, a separate MS Access database was sufficient, even though the manual transfer of data was tedious. However, when the project grew and the files became large, it was a huge challenge for one staff member to handle the data transfer and updating tasks. E-Reserve turned to the library's programming staff for help with creating a database that would alleviate the situation. More recently, other options were explored, including conducting a feasibility study of commercial systems such as Atlas' Ares and Docutek's ERes. Of course, the cost of acquiring another system and also how effectively the system interacts with the existing process are big considerations. During the online meeting of Ontario e-reserve librarians and staff in February 2009, the University of Guelph librarian stated the need to acquire an e-reserve system to manage the copyright process. Their e-reserve project has grown to such a magnitude that no ordinary separate files could cope with the large amount of file data and analysis. They have chosen Ares because it is designed mainly for e-reserve applications. Though U.S.-based, the system seems flexible enough for customization to local needs. Ares is open to modifying the system for the Canadian environment, such as a direct gateway to Access Copyright, the Canadian counterpart of the U.S. Copyright Clearance Center, as well as offering a separate component to handle direct dealings with individual publishers.

Formats and digitizing issues

One of the biggest problems that digital technology has created for the e-reserve process is the increased complication and time required in obtaining permissions for online access to copyrighted materials. In multimedia documents, there can be multiple copyright owners and layers of copyright to be cleared in a piece of work – images, audio or video clips, photographs, the performance itself and the music. Each and every one of these rights holders has to be approached for permissions to use their work legally. The Canadian Copyright Act contains a statutory exception for LAMS (libraries, archives and museums) and educational institutions. However, these exceptions are not helpful in addressing issues specific to streaming. Jean Dryden, a copyright specialist in Canada, discussed 'Copyright issues in audio- and video-streaming' on 12 February 2008, at an Education Institute Web conference in Canada. She explained that first, the exceptions apply only to copies for research or private study or preservation, and secondly, the part on transmission of data refers only to radio or television broadcasting to students at the time of broadcast. In her opinion, streaming to a class is probably not fair dealing because it does not meet the purpose or character criteria. Streaming to individuals at a time of their choosing may be fair dealing.

Faculty can request any electronic formats of materials to be put on e-reserve, as long as they comply with copyright. The CAUL survey (Poleykett, 2003) reported that 20% of the Australian library respondents provided audio visual materials on their e-reserves. These were mostly digital recordings of lectures. One library digitized the recordings and hosted them in-house whereas another library provided links to materials digitized by another unit in the university. Results from the December 2008 Ryerson University survey (Appendix I) indicated that scanned files (PDF) were the most popular requests (89%). Links to databases (80%), links to Websites (76%) and links to e-books (71%) were the next choice, followed by Word, Excel or PowerPoint files (57%). As far as streaming is concerned, in-house streamed video (25%) or audio (25%) were more common than linking to streamed audio (16%) or video databases (19%). Multimedia playlists (7%), learning objects (10%) and podcasts (5%) were only starting to emerge.

To avoid the copyright permission process, libraries may look for pre-cleared licensed uses of audiovisual content from sources such as the Creative Commons and Flickr. There are also specific licenses on Websites, such as CBC's (Canadian Broadcasting Corporation) terms of use, which permit certain streaming. Publishers are offering custom-made online teaching materials for interactive applications. Pearson Custom Publishing, found at *www.pearsoncustom.com/database*, advertises its database of online copyright-cleared content and media services, including CD, DVD, e-books and companion Websites, for faculty to build their own textbook, casebook, reader or manual for classroom. As well as selecting chapters from textbooks available from the publisher, instructors can add their own material, students' work, or materials from third-party sources to put together with this content. The materials are then delivered through flash-based simulations or tutorials, PowerPoint slides, videos or animated presentations on a wide selection of platforms, including CD-ROM, DVD, Websites and portals, or a course management system. The latter is powered by Blackboard and includes its features of online assessment such as test and quiz questions, and communication tools such as announcements, email, discussion boards, chat rooms and personal student pages. Institutions can select from a variety of costing models – individual purchase of passwords by students, licensing to departments or to the whole campus.

Online Companions to textbooks are available. VangoNotes, found at *http://www.audible.com/adbl/store/btq/vangonotes/home.jsp?BV_UseBVCookie=Yes*, is a joint venture of textbook publisher Pearson Education, found at *http://www.pearsoned.com/* and digital audio content distributor Audible Inc., found at *http://www.audible.com*. These are downloadable audio study guides tied to textbooks to explain, chapter by chapter, the content, the key concepts and terminology, and provide practice test for review. Pricing is done at the chapter level or the complete set, downloadable on computers or MP3 players.

Cdigix, a Seattle-based company in the United States, was a company focused on selling a service to colleges and universities to place movies or music on reserve online for students. The company ceased operation in early 2009 on the alleged reasons of the poor economy (Young, 2009). At one point in time, about 25 to 30 U.S. colleges, large and small, signed up for the program or tested the product. One condition was the libraries had to own a hard copy. Libraries sent to the company any media materials such as videos and DVD that they wanted to digitize. C-Labs, the company's service, digitized the material and provided a server and the technology to prepare the videos with DRM (Digital Rights Management) protection to prevent further distribution. Faculty and students were then able to download the online materials, but not to stream. The platforms used to view were Windows Media or Real Player. What about copyright? In spite of the provisions of the U.S. Teach Act of 2003, there were doubts among librarians about the legality of placing copyrighted works online for reserve, though with restricted access by students in the course.

How copyright impacts on staff interaction with faculty

In 2006, the American Association of Publishers threatened to sue Cornell University in the United States for violating the copyright law in its posting of copyrighted materials on its course Website. Rice (2006) reported on new copyright compliance guidelines compiled by Cornell because of the threat of a lawsuit. The guidelines were said to have no 'dramatic differences' from prior practice. The university bookstore was still responsible for clearing copyright for print course packs and students needed to pay to purchase these materials. Faculty were responsible for making sure that materials posted at their own course Websites or within Blackboard were copyright cleared. With e-reserve, the library required that all the proper permissions were obtained before materials would be posted but did not police the professors. Nonetheless, the threat of a lawsuit with regard to copyright infringement has heightened campus awareness of the need to clear copyright, even for educational purposes. Cornell drafted a new policy to provide faculty with guidance on how to determine if copyright permission was required when posting course materials. Faculty were provided with a checklist for conducting a fair use analysis before using copyright materials (Bridges, 2007).

The Cornell case illustrates the importance of promoting copyright awareness to the community served by an educational institution. A frequently asked copyright question is: can we copy from the Internet? Noel (2005), a Canadian lawyer, reminded teachers that most materials on the Internet, such as postings of newsgroups, emails, images, photographs, music and video clips, and computer software, are protected by copyright, and unauthorized uses are prohibited. While copyright protects the expression of information, the information itself is not under copyright. Therefore, restating ideas or facts in one's own words does not infringe copyright. However, one has to be careful with statements about free use of works on the Internet. She pointed out there is often an actual license to copy under some conditions. These conditions include the purpose of use – not for commercial or for-profit, or circulation in its entirety, without modifications or editing. If permissions are required from the copyright owner, Noel emphasized the importance of putting the request in writing.

These are useful guidelines that should be shared with faculty when organizing materials for their course Websites, which often include Internet materials. The questions are when and how. We have heard comments like 'students don't read signs'. The same may also be said of faculty who do not want to peruse guidelines either in print or on the library's Web page before requesting the service. Even if they have read part of the content, they still maintain that digital copying for the sake of education and controlled access through devices such as logins to a course management system would be good enough. E-reserve staff should be knowledgeable enough to answer these challenges from faculty and tactful enough to turn down requests deemed to be not compliant with copyright law.

Linking: technical issues and methods

Why link?

In print-based reserve services, libraries generally place entire books on reserve, or copy portions of text and journal articles to be placed on reserve as reprints. The equivalent of this in an electronic reserve environment would be to upload PDF files to an e-reserve system that could then be accessed by students enrolled in a course. However, this is often not possible.

The vendor license agreement terms that academic libraries must abide by in Canada (though the majority of academic library vendors are based in the United States), usually do not allow the creation of a locally stored digital copy of subscribed or purchased electronic content.

Ryerson's e-resource collection, as in many academic institutions today, is a combination of purchased journal backfiles, subscription based electronic journal collections, aggregator products, publisher platforms for individually subscribed e-journals, portals and more. Because of the restrictive nature of many of these vendors' license terms, as well as the wide variety of acceptable usage vis-à-vis downloading and storage of online content, the library is not permitted to upload PDF files to be stored on a local server (although it is technically possible with Blackboard and other e-reserve systems). Because of this limitation, the library is left with a second-best option: to create links to readings on the publisher or vendor's site that students use to access their reserve materials.

Complexities of linking

In order to create a link to a subscribed or purchased e-resource for use in reading lists, the person creating the link must include two ingredients.

The first ingredient is the library's proxy (or other authentication method) information and the second ingredient is a persistent URL for accessing the resource. Free e-resources are also sometimes included in reading lists, so these would not require authentication, but still require a persistent URL.

The Ryerson Library, as well as all of the other 20 member institutions within the Ontario Council of University Libraries (OCUL) consortium, authenticates patrons for access to online resources based on Internet protocol (IP) address whenever possible. Each university has an IP range or ranges that they register with all vendors who are equipped to authenticate users based on IP address. On the university campus(es), all computers in the library, campus computer labs, and faculty and staff offices, have an IP address within the institution's IP range(s). Therefore, all on campus access to the IP-authenticated, electronic resources can occur directly. In contrast, off campus users will not have IP addresses within the institution's range, so that another product is needed to provide those authorized users (generally limited to current students, faculty and staff members), with IP access to the content to which they are entitled remote access. For this purpose, the libraries utilize a proxy server to route legitimate off-campus traffic. The proxy server has an IP address within the institution's range. Users have a login and password, generally for a campus computing-wide set of credentials, to enter when going through the proxy, and once logged in they appear at the vendor's site to have the IP address of the proxy server and are allowed to access the electronic content. To provide a sense of how many libraries utilize this authentication method, one of the most popular proxy server products on the market, EZproxy, boasts customers including more than 2,500 institutions in over 60 countries (OCLC Online Computer Library Center, Inc., 2009).

In order to route the electronic resource traffic through the proxy, URLs for each product, along with any other required setup configuration, are added to the institution's proxy table, and then a proxy prefix, or rewrite, is added to the resource URLs in catalogue links, library Website links, e-reserve links, and to any other access point which is provided for the institution's patrons. If this rewrite, or prefix, has not been added to the database URLs, any patron attempting to access that resource from off-campus will not be permitted to access the resources at the vendor's site. Because most students have computers at home which they use for their coursework as well as for leisure, it is vitally important that any links provided for them include the proxy rewrite. At the same time, it is very easy for faculty members, and even staff, to neglect to include the proxy rewrite, because on-campus access to the resources is automatically IP authenticated without the proxy rewrite. It may appear that the link is working perfectly on campus, but off-campus users encounter an error or a *not subscribed* message when attempting to access the resource.

The persistent URL method

Persistent URLs (PURLS), also referred to as durable or stable URLs, are defined as,

> Permanent identifiers in the face of a dynamic and changing Web infrastructure. Instead of resolving directly to Web resources (documents, data, services, people, etc.) [they] provide a level of indirection that allows the underlying Web addresses of resources to change over time without negatively affecting systems that depend on them. (OCLC Online Computer Library Center, Inc., n.d)

PURLS are required so that students can get to their readings reliably, as long as the library continues its subscription to those resources. URLs that work today are subject to structural changes made by vendors. The use of URLs copied from a browser's address bar is insufficient for e-reserve purposes, because these URLs can change at any time, often without warning, and usually it is a student or faculty member attempting to read their course materials, rather than a library staff member, who finds the error. This results in user dissatisfaction, and leads to a negative impression of e-reserve services.

Some vendors have made the process of capturing a persistent URL relatively simple for those who know what they are looking for. For example, two of Ryerson's major aggregated database vendors, ProQuest and EBSCO, include a field in all of their database records that will link the user back to that specific item. Notice in the figures below that Ryerson's EZproxy rewrite (*http://ezproxylib.ryerson.ca/login?url=*) is included in the persistent URL. If this field is utilized to copy the URL, it will work properly both on campus and off campus. However, if the browser's address bar is used as the source for copying the URL, this will not work once that particular database session has ended.

Gale, a third aggregated database vendor popular among North American Academic library customers, offers a persistent link field in their databases, but has not set it up to work as reliably as ProQuest or EBSCO. Gale's field, called Bookmark, contains a persistent link to that

Figure 6.2	ProQuest's Document URL field contains a persistent URL for that item. If the site administrator has set it up, the library's proxy information is also incorporated into the PURL

Figure 6.3	EBSCO's Persistent link (Permalink) field contains a persistent URL to that item. As with ProQuest, if the site administrator has set it up, the library's proxy information is added to the PURL

item, but only includes the institution's proxy rewrite information if the user has accessed Gale from off campus. This means that if a library staff member, or faculty member, has accessed the database from their office on campus, the link will need to be edited to include the proxy rewrite in order for the link to work for off-campus users.

These vendors' efforts do not make the process seamless, but they very much improve the ease of creating links to documents – by library staff, and also for end users. Many other vendors and e-journal publishers provide no such field or help information for creating persistent URLs, so that Ryerson Library had to create extensive instructions for generating these links for the many database vendors.

The DOI method

An alternative to creating a persistent link to an item based on the vendor's site guidelines or PURL field, is to use a Digital Object Identifier (DOI) (*http://www.doi.org/*). The DOI system is an ISO registered standard and was designed as a persistent identification method for online objects. Objects can be online journals, articles, books, book chapters, and other types of content. DOIs and the services that they can be used to enable are broader than those discussed here. Interested readers may pursue this topic further at *http://www.doi.org/*. Registration agencies like CrossRef assist publishers in assigning persistent DOI names for their content for linking, marketing, and tracking purposes. As expressed on the DOI Website, 'information about a digital object may change over time, including where to find it, but its DOI name will not change' (*http://www.doi.org/*).

By 2008, DOIs had been assigned to over 40 million articles (Paskin, 2010), and as of August 2009, 2845 publishers and societies had registered with CrossRef for DOI prefixes ('CrossRef Indicators', 2009). For a few important reasons, DOIs, as with persistent URLs, are helpful only for those who are knowledgeable about where to find them and how to use them.

First, a DOI name alone is not enough information for linking to that item. In order to link to an object using the DOI name, the link creator must express that DOI as an URL. The means for accomplishing this is to add the DOI system proxy server: http://dx.doi.org ahead of the DOI name. So, in order to link to the item with the DOI name 10.1007/3-540-45747-X_23, one would need to form the URL http://dx.doi.org/10.1007/3-540-45747-X_23. Most publishers who assign DOI names to their content include a DOI field in their online platforms, and some indexing services also include a DOI name field, but the DOI proxy server information is not generally included.

Second, the DOI name plus DOI server proxy prefix still requires the library's proxy rewrite in order to create links to purchased or subscribed materials that facilitate off-campus access. In Ryerson's case, the link created above would then need to become: *http://ezproxy.lib.ryerson.ca/login?url*=http://dx.doi.org/10.1007/3-540-45747-X_23.

Third, the person creating the link needs to be able to distinguish whether the site at which they have located their item and corresponding DOI is the publisher's site. Either this, or they would need to be sure to test the link and confirm full text access is possible from that location. Because the DOI prefix is assigned to a particular publisher, links using DOI names will resolve to the publisher's full text platform. Because indexing and full text database providers as well as publisher platforms include DOI fields, it is quite possible to locate full text within an aggregated database, create a link using the DOI, but then not access the institution's full text for that item using the DOI URL. This would happen if the library has access to that item through an aggregated database, but not at the journal publisher's own site. This last consideration poses the greatest challenge in creating instructions or providing training for creating persistent links using the DOI. Even library staff members can find it difficult to distinguish between different types of electronic resource platforms. It may not be clear to the person creating the link whether what they have located is a publisher site, an aggregated database, or some other type of resource.

The primary barrier to faculty self-sufficiency in creating reading lists that connect students to their required and recommended online readings is the difficulty of creating persistent URLs.

The OpenURL method

In contrast to the persistent URL and DOI linking methods described above, whose utilization depends upon the location of the full text item requiring a link, OpenURL links can be generated using standard steps regardless of the full text resource type. OpenURL1.0 is a NISO standard (ANSI/NISO Z39.88) that uses metadata to construct context sensitive URLs. Libraries can implement OpenURL link resolvers to present relevant resources available to its users for requested items at the time of need. Available items are controlled by means of a knowledge base, or database of current library subscriptions and purchases that the link resolver company and customers keep up-to-date. They work in conjunction with the library's chosen authentication method so that available items are also defined according to which resources a particular user has access to at the moment he or she requests them through the OpenURL link or button. Some examples of OpenURL link resolvers currently on the market include Innovative Interfaces' Webbridge, ExLibris' SFX, and Serials Solutions' 360 Link. Depending on the library's selection and needs, the OpenURL link resolver can be integrated with their ILS system (Webbridge integrated with Innovative ILS for example) or can stand alone (SFX can be used by any ILS user, though Ex Libris also has an ILS on the market).

OpenURL linking occurs as follows. OpenURL enabled sources send item metadata to the OpenURL link resolver. The resolver then checks the metadata against the customer's knowledge base to determine whether full text is available, and then displays full text sources that are available to the user. The proxy information is automatically added to the resource if appropriate, and provided the user has off-campus access to electronic resources, they can then link to the full text resource.

Library customers with OpenURL link resolvers in place can register their OpenURL details with all OpenURL compliant database vendors so that citations in indexing databases connect with currently available full text where the library has an active subscription or owned full text. Also, some free sources such as Google Scholar are interoperable with OpenURL resolvers. They also generally come with a journals by title a–z list and a method for generating e-journal catalogue records (an example of this is Ex Libris' Marc-It! service for SFX customers).

The primary benefits of using the OpenURL method are:

- Access and subscription details are maintained in one central knowledge base. Changes made to the knowledge base such as added or dropped titles, and new resource locations are reflected right away without the need to edit a link.
- One method can be used by e-reserve staff for creating all links.
- Users are provided with a familiar access route whether accessing electronic resources from e-reserve, the library catalogue, a–z list, or indexing databases.
- OpenURL resolvers offer library branding opportunity, so that students know the library is providing the access, and that it is not just free to anyone.

Because many electronic resources such as free electronic journals and aggregated database vendor's title offerings change over time, and because publisher's titles sometimes also get taken over by other publishers, the ability to maintain available titles and e-products in a central spot is a huge benefit. Existing OpenURL links automatically provide current access options to authorized users when the knowledge base is updated.

Ryerson, along with all of the other OCUL libraries, are using SFX. SFX includes a citation linker and also an OpenURL generator, either of which can be used to input an article or e-book's metadata and get an OpenURL back. The OpenURL can then be copied and pasted into an e-reserve system and will never have to be edited as long as the library continues to use SFX. The only reason to alter the OpenURL is if the library stops subscribing or loses access to that particular item through all available sources. Even in this case, the user does not encounter an error message, but rather a message that the resource is not available at their institution, and is then presented with an opportunity to submit an interlibrary loan request for their item (see Figure 6.4).

Figure 6.4   SFX menu showing Interlibrary Loan option

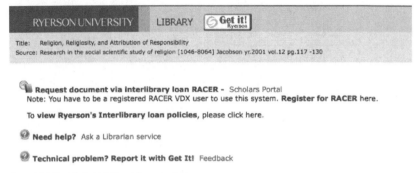

Copyright Ex Libris Ltd. Used by permission.

In the case of broken links, the technical support staff that maintains the OpenURL knowledge base resolves the problem centrally, so that all links to that item, from e-reserve and from all other access points, are fixed in a single step.

Once users are familiar with the OpenURL linking process, they are generally satisfied with it. However, as mentioned in Chapter 7, OpenURL linking does not always meet user's expectations – from within e-reserve, and also in general. Because of the wide variety of vendors whose products make up our electronic resources collection, the linking experience varies. Several vendors' sites are configured so that incoming OpenURL links can take the user directly to the full text article location. Libraries who are members of CrossRef, and who are SFX customers, can optimize some additional vendors' sites for OpenURL linking through the use of DOIs, as the DOI can often take the user closer to the article level than would otherwise be possible. Other vendors do not possess the technical capability to link at this level, and users are delivered farther away from their article, to perhaps an article issue, journal homepage, or even a database homepage. This can be a frustrating experience for users who have already searched a database, and then find themselves having to search for their specific article again. E-reserve users have expressed this frustration, as eloquently stated by some of the distance education undergraduates utilizing a course reserve in 2007. They expressed a desire for a 'direct link to the article posted in the course E-reserve page' that 'eliminates the need to search and search for the article'. SFX as originally designed displays a menu of choices to the user depending on the OpenURL provided and available choices defined by the library in their knowledge base. This means that OpenURLs in e-reserve first take users to a menu of choices, from which they are required to choose an option. Even if the first full text option on the menu directly sends the user to the article page, this creates an additional click not encountered when a persistent URL to the article has been provided. Any extra clicks or steps generally detract from the user's positive perception of the service.

In recent years, however, Ex Libris has introduced a DirectLink feature for SFX that can be enabled by libraries to eliminate the menu display when full text (or other services as defined by the customer) is available. When DirectLink is activated for SFX, the OpenURL takes the user directly to the full text target instead of displaying the menu.

Ryerson library is currently testing the DirectLink feature (see Figure 6.5), and intends to share the results of a user survey regarding the user

Figure 6.5   **SFX DirectLink banner with article below**

Copyright Ex Libris Ltd. Used by permission.

Figure 6.6   **SFX menu for the OpenURL request in Figure 6.4**

Copyright Ex Libris Ltd. Used by permission.

experience of DirectLink. The authors anticipate that the drawbacks of using OpenURL for e-reserve will decrease as a result of activating the DirectLink feature.

In summary, the process of creating links that will work for a population using computers from both on and off campus is currently rather complicated, and is not easily transferable from library staff to faculty members. While the steps for creating OpenURL links are standard, this is not the type of link faculty members always desire. Some very technologically savvy and library resource literate faculty members may be able to create their own persistent links, but most will require assistance from library staff to make their electronic reading lists function properly.

User perception and satisfaction

Copyright related

In addition to having to comply with copyright laws that are often awkward in application, libraries also have to deal with users' lack of understanding of copyright in the digital environment. Chapter 1 has described the Millennial generation of users and their behavior – the desire for connectivity, interactivity, individuality and portability and the impatience for settling for anything less than immediate fulfillment of their information needs. 24/7, real time, anytime and anywhere access are terms that we are all too familiar with. This desire for fast return of information search results is not limited to the younger students who grew up with the Internet, laptops, notebooks and cell phones. Today's faculty are also demanding a similar speed in retrieving information, in getting to the full content (not an abstract or summary or another reference to the full text) right away. Faculty and students alike refuse to be persuaded that copyright is not impeding free access to information. To them, copyright seems to be a non-issue in cyber space. We hear our faculty and students ask why they cannot link to any Web page and incorporate it into their own works, whether it is for an assignment, a term paper, a course page, a publication or a class presentation? If people allow others to see their page on the Web, is that not an indication that they want it to be shared? The strongest argument used by faculty and students is fair use, fair dealing or the teaching and educational environment. They feel that if the purpose of using a document or a video clip is for non-commercial, non-profit use, is it not a good reason for exemption from copyright payment to the authors or publishers? They do not understand the distinction between classroom use and private research, since both are for the purpose of education and teaching and learning. They question, even given the risk factor, how many times libraries and academic institutions have been sued for infringing copyright due to copying from the Internet? How frequently have individuals – teachers or students – been caught in legal battles over digital copying of Web materials for their academic output? In the case of using a course management system, students or class access are already limited by the login and password process. Again, they ask, is the dealing or use not fair enough, since information is not widely distributed? Rice (2006) reported on the pressure put on Cornell University by the American Association of Publishers to change its e-reserve practice. The association maintained that the university's posting of copyrighted materials on its course Website was in violation of the copyright law. Commenting on the problem, the university's Copyright Compliance Officer explained that the problem was largely due to faculty's misunderstanding or lack of knowledge about electronic media. 'Faculty are now where students were five years ago with Napster. Just because it's easy to take something on a Website does not mean it's legal to do so.' Technically possible does *not* mean that it is legally permissible.

E-reserve faculty users are often of the opinion that fair use (United States) or fair dealing (Canada) will permit them to post copyrighted materials online, for instruction and learning purposes. They think that exceptions will be made in an educational setting, especially if the material is posted in a course management system that restricts access to students enrolled in the course. It is true that legislation recognizes that certain rights to the use of copyrighted materials must be extended to users engaged in research and creative activities. There are provisions in copyright acts that intended to balance the interest of the creators and owners of works on one side and the legitimate rights of the users on the other side. Unfortunately, what is meant by fair use or fair dealing in the legal context is not always clear. The court of law actually makes the final determination of what use or dealing is fair.

It is difficult for libraries or e-reserve staff to explain the complexity of the digital copyright environment to an audience who is not enthusiastic in the least to listen. Meanwhile, libraries are aware that faculty, impatient to wait for the copyright clearance process or confident enough with their education and fair use or fair dealing argument, will dismiss e-reserve altogether and prepare their own course readings. Having once encountered slow response time from copyright owners or the hefty payment demanded, they may either go back to print course packs or resort to their own fair use or fair dealing argument and incorporate the information in their own Web pages, at most password controlled, to students enrolled in their classes.

One-stop searching, single sign-on and direct link to document

Faculty and students are so used to the Google method of searching for information that their tolerance level for anything less easy and simple is minimal. How many times have we heard students say why cannot libraries group all the resources – books, articles, videos – in one place, or in one database, and allow them to search using words they are familiar with? Why should they have to learn to formulate a search statement, with Boolean operators *and*, *or* and *not* or truncation symbols? Even if they do not have to actually type those characters, why should they have to understand the logic behind them and fill in their search words in the appropriate fields? Why cannot there be one single search box, as they see on the Google page?

If e-reserve is within a course management system, and remote library access requires another log-in step with a different account and password, the frustration is even more acute. Before EZproxy was implemented by Ryerson Library in December 2007, remote access to library databases required an intermediary step of library authentication by the library barcode (a 12-digit number) and a PIN (last 4 digits of the staff/student code). Making users understand where to locate the barcode on their library cards and where to extract the PIN was not an easy task. It was even more difficult to accommodate the requests of Distance Education students, who were not automatically assigned the barcodes and PIN. It was a chore for library staff as well as a nuisance for students. In those days, when a Ryerson student wanted to access E-Reserve in Blackboard from home or office, s/he had to first log in to Blackboard. In order to access the links to articles in library subscribed databases, s/he had to go past the library barcode/PIN authentication, using an account and a password which was different from Blackboard's.

Users these days are accustomed to being one click away from full content. If the link to an article does not get them to the full text but presents another menu with database choices or a chronological list of volumes and issues that requires further navigation, they are not buying in. Ryerson University Library E-Reserve participated in two Distance Education end-of-term student surveys in March and November 2007 (Appendix V). The full details of these two surveys will be discussed in Chapter 7 on possible strategies and the importance of evaluation and assessment. Apart from quantitative data, answers to the open-ended question are helpful in understanding students' perceptions of the service and their ideas for improvement. There were repeated remarks on the difficulty of searching, the inconvenience of waiting for an assigned library barcode and the failure of a direct link to the document itself. Direct link to the articles without another authentication was most frequently mentioned. Below are a few examples of such comments:

'Not having to go through 2–3 or even sometimes 4 different "windows" to view what I want to see/read …'

'Direct link between article posted in the course to E-Reserve page.'

'… Eliminates the need to search and search for the article.'

The removal of the barcode/PIN authentication access to library resources from remote access in December 2007 was a big triumph in winning over user support. It was of no surprise that users voluntarily wrote to the library blog to support the change after the implementation of EZproxy.

Nonetheless, single sign-on has not removed all other points of frustration with e-reserve access. The term e-reserve is a known problem. On the Ryerson Library Web page, the term Course Readings is now used as an alternative to Reserve for catalogue search. However, in other areas of the Web pages, in other library official publications, and the service counter itself, Reserve is still the term being used. E-Reserve, the electronic equivalent, continues this tradition in all its advertising to the faculty and communication with other university counterparts, who also seem to uphold the terminology. Proprietary systems such as Docutek's ERes and Atlas' Ares are assuming the reserve stem word. Course management system such as Blackboard also uses eReserves to name the module. Widespread as the term is, users do not seem to understand the meaning and its functions. Reserve is often confused with putting a hold on material. As the electronic links in e-reserve look similar to what users see when they search library databases, electronic resource and reserve are synonymous in their minds. That has implications on how they look for e-reserve readings. In Ryerson's case, since library staff create the readings on behalf of faculty, the most usual way for faculty to incorporate these in Blackboard is to create a sub-folder within their course page called e-reserve, so that library staff can load the links into this subfolder. This eliminates the need for them to copy and paste individual links in the course text. When students open up the link to their course, they will have to know that the readings are in a folder called e-reserve. In some instances, faculty may have other sub-folders called Course Documents or Course Notes, which may make more sense to the students for locating course-related readings than e-reserve. A click on Ryerson's e-reserve link will bring up another page with the course name and e-reserve file extension and a couple of warning messages about remote access and Adobe Acrobat for PDF viewing. Students sometimes were at a loss for what to do next, not knowing they needed another click on a link to get to another screen with more folders that contain the course readings. There were at least three clicks before they could see the titles of the documents, and sometimes, a few more clicks before the actual full text appeared.

Library terminology and intuitive interface

Too often, one tends to blame the system for not being user-friendly or intuitive. In the example above, human decision plays a part in the design. Ryerson E-Reserve has had enough feedback from surveys or word-of-mouth comments about the confusion over the e-reserve folder in the Blackboard navigation bar and the intervening information page about authentication and Adobe software requirement. It is high time the practice be reviewed and a more intuitive interface be put in place. One idea would be to rename the folder to something students understand immediately, such as Required Readings or Course Readings. E-Reserve can also remove the intervening page and think of ways that students can land on the documents right away after one click on the Course Readings folder. E-Reserve is reviewing the use of the SFX menu for multiple database display, in collaboration with the Digital Support Librarian for the overall decision on what to display when a user searches the library databases for locating an article. The choice is between seeing a direct link to the document from a pre-determined database, with only a back-up screen of other alternatives, or maintaining the current menu of a multiple choice of databases for the same article, along with the library branding. The former involves an evaluation of the reliability and performance of specific databases and the quality of the display, but the latter promotes the library's involvement in the process.

Submitting requests

Another user perception that e-reserve staff have to deal with happens at the stage of faculty submitting their requests (this may be less of a problem for institutions using a dedicated system). Faculty requests and personal data are more likely to go into a database where staff can act upon. When, however, the requests come in the form of unformatted email or just data in a Web form that ends up in a staff email account, problems begin to surface if staff receive a large volume of requests. Communication back and forth with faculty over the copyright permission process aggravates the problem, as staff will have to search through these emails to trace the flow of the same request. Staff have to deal with inadequate or sometimes inaccurate citations provided by faculty, so Ryerson Library has a Web form with structured fields and sample citations for faculty to follow. Rarely do faculty complete those forms. Emails consisting of cut and paste citations are the most common. What can be done to persuade faculty to use the form when they think they have provided the library with complete information necessary for processing?

Marketing and faculty reaction to new service

Ryerson Library's marketing of RefShare to faculty for creating their own electronic readings reveals another issue that is more human than technical. Faculty were very receptive of RefWorks as a bibliographic management tool. They encouraged students to attend library workshops and had assignments that required students to make use of the software. However, when it came to RefShare, which is only one step further, to share their research readings with students, similar to e-reserve readings, little or no progress was made. Many promotional efforts have been taken, through workshops and disseminating the information on faculty listservs, and a Camtasia video was produced showing how simple the process was. Nevertheless, no one has yet approached E-Reserve to enquire about the piloted use of RefShare for creating online readings.

However, there are success cases at other institutions. York University and Nippissing University in Ontario, Canada are two institutions that use RefWorks for creating electronic reading lists. One distinction between their practices and Ryerson's pilot project was that RefWorks was the only option offered and library staff actually created the links and sent to faculty. Ryerson was hoping to market RefShare as a faculty do-it-yourself option. No study has been undertaken to ascertain to what extent the inertia was due to unwillingness to learn another tool or the fact that faculty were content with library staff doing all the work for them. Nonetheless, what the Library highlighted as one of the main selling points of RefShare, the added value of correct citations and ability to interact with students on a specific document, did not seem attractive enough for faculty to change their habit of requesting library staff to create e-reserve links on their behalf.

7

Possible strategies

Collaboration, integration and interaction are the keystones for survival or expansion of e-reserve service

In the face of constant new developments in the technological environment, the best strategy for e-reserve service is to embrace change, look for opportunities to collaborate with other teaching and learning partners inside and outside the institution, and integrate with other campus services to provide the holistic education experience that the new generation of users demand. The December 2008 survey conducted by Ryerson University librarians had a question on 'collaboration with others outside the library' (Appendix I); 39% answered in the positive. The majority of these collaborations were with the university's IT department and mainly for audio or video streaming initiatives, followed by Blackboard staff for technical support. The next area of collaboration was with distance education or open learning. Lastly, e-reserve operations worked along with departments that support teaching or with teaching faculty and individual academic departments. One U.S. institution respondent was emphatic about partnerships.

> Innovative Interfaces is [the] entry point for reserves, has print reserves, links to ERes and links to e-books for some courses ... The University has a hodge-podge of methods for providing access to course materials. These include bookstore, library reserves, course Websites, podcasts, course packs ... just about anything you can think of ... We view course reserves as a means to an end. If another method would be more effective, we refer faculty there. For example, we work closely with the staff that produce course packs. They have access to information about our licenses so that they know which

materials are already licensed by the libraries for inclusion in course packs, reducing the cost of course packs for students … We view ERes as just one part of a system of providing access to course materials. We spend a lot of time educating library reserves processing staff about alternatives so that we can be effective partners in education.

Collaboration and partnerships are important. So is interaction with users. To ensure that the library service is satisfying users' needs, e-reserve administrators have to find out what faculty and students really want via surveys, focus groups or other methods of soliciting feedback.

The importance of evaluation and assessment

Poe (2006) at Houston Cole Library, Jacksonville State University in the United States, described various methods in marketing electronic reserves at her university library. She emphasized the importance of creating a written marketing plan to ensure the successful introduction of a new service. Her plan included using the university's email system to make initial contact with students, faculty, and staff; a flyer advertising the service to be distributed to all students; and, at the beginning of each semester, a message sent to the formal liaison network that the library has established and to faculty teaching distance education courses. To ensure that service goals are met, she recommended undertaking two surveys – one for faculty and one for students. The survey should ask specific questions about the awareness and use of the system, and some open-ended questions to solicit feedback on how to better market the system.

In addition to marketing the service, finding out users' needs and satisfaction through surveys is a good strategy. Detailed analysis and following up on survey findings is essential. Austin and Taylor (2007) described their first attempt at assessing electronic reserve service at the University of Colorado in the United States. The survey results confirmed that the project was a success. Two important findings helped to determine the future direction of library reserve services. First, a majority of students (74.2%) preferred electronic reserves to paper reserves. Secondly, electronic reserves were preferred to course packs (54.5% to 34.3%). Free-text responses to a question 'What did you like LEAST about electronic reserves' were particularly useful in obtaining suggestions for service improvement.

According to Austin and Taylor, the benefits from this survey went beyond the assessment process and data collected as a closer relationship with faculty members was established since such interaction. The library was seen as being responsive to user needs. Unexpected partnerships with other campus units, such as the Bookstore and Imaging Services, were formed, when these units expressed interest in the survey results. Above all, student feedback on course packs versus print and electronic reserves led the institution to think of ways to merge these services, in order to provide one-stop shopping for users, faculty and students alike.

Assessment is an important part of any library service, including electronic reserves. Unfortunately, libraries do not always find the time to carry out a well-designed survey. The 2005 Seneca College survey of Canadian e-reserve operations revealed that:

> The lack of statistics is the first obvious void. Statistics often quantify a library's existence and the absence of statistics is a little surprising. Marketing plans were also almost non-existent. There were a few schools that seemed to have a plan of attack for launching and supporting their e-reserves initiatives but many just relied on word of mouth. (Peters-Lise et al., 2006)

Ryerson University librarians' more recent survey in 2008 of mainly North American libraries also indicated that assessment and evaluation were heavily reliant on word-of-mouth rather than formal surveys or focus groups (Appendix I).

The University of Waterloo in Ontario, Canada surveyed their faculty in 2002 to assess their satisfaction with current reserve service before planning improvements (Ferster et al., 2006). A companion survey was done in 2004 to obtain students' perceptions of service (Leonard et al., 2006). The student survey had a 23% response rate from a random sample of 5,000 students, which represented reasonably well the opinions of the student population. A number of recommendations for the future directions of the service were based on analysis of these findings. The survey discovered that 38% of e-reserve student users accessed the readings via the e-reserve database page, whereas 62% used the library catalogue course reserve area. This resulted in the continuation of two e-reserve searching options, specifically the e-reserve database and the library catalogue. There was an interesting divide between faculty's and students' perspectives. While faculty indicated a significant need for the library to continue the traditional print reserve that includes books, and copyrighted journal articles, students clearly preferred electronic access (43% preferred e-reserve and 7% paper reserve). Nevertheless, the report indicated that other important changes had taken place since the 2002 faculty survey, and there was sufficient evidence to believe that electronic delivery of reserve content has become more accepted by faculty. The report noted that the popularity of the university's course content system (increased from a few courses to over 500 courses reaching 20,000 students) was a major development that contributed to the change in faculty's attitude. Another significant development was the adoption of electronic delivery of reserve materials by the Distance Education department. The report suggested a re-assessment of the library's role in delivering course-specific content beyond e-reserve, naming examples such as electronic subject guides and reference sources to offer a coherent package of course-specific information integrated with the course management system.

Ryerson University Library started its E-Reserve service in 2004, a few years later than the University of Waterloo. As a late starter, Ryerson enjoyed the advantage of learning from predecessors. A faculty survey was carried out in May 2005, shortly after launching the E-Reserve pilot (Appendix II). The questionnaire was directed at about 200 faculty members who used Print Reserve and E-Reserve. Thirty-four faculty members (20%) responded online (60% used Print Reserve only, 16% used E-Reserve exclusively and 24% used both Print and E-Reserve). The day program instructors were more inclined to respond (85%). Print Reserve received very good ratings for overall satisfaction (59% excellent; 16% very good). Ninety-four per cent of E-Reserve users said they would use the E-Reserve service again, but numbers were split on whether they preferred to use Blackboard for E-Reserve (56% less willing; 44% more willing). Users were happy with processing time for E-Reserve and staff help in both Print and E-Reserve services. Interestingly, there were some very good as well as bad ratings for the ease of placing requests, for both Print and E-Reserve. Satisfaction with the paper request forms for Print Reserve was much higher than using the online form. As a result of this survey, it was decided that the paper Print Reserve request form would remain, as users preferred submitting requests in that way. The online form was reviewed as well as the submitting process. A fair number of faculty did not use E-Reserve and the reasons cited were:

Never heard of it – 40%

Materials not suitable for E-Reserve – 40%

Others – 24%

Preference for Print Reserve – 16%

Takes too long to clear copyright – 8%

Copyright costs too high – 4%

Technical problems – 4%

Not user-friendly – 0%.

The top two reasons were 'never heard of it' or 'materials not suitable'. There were some very revealing answers in the open-ended questions section. Faculty who tried E-Reserve and liked it were saying 'it would simplify the process of finding reserve material for the students'; 'this is a wonderful service and [I] would never go back to a reprotext. The support and service I have received from the team was amazing. The students stated this as well. I use this with 3 courses I lead and this year alone over 1000+ accessed the E resource and comments were very positive'; 'I used it for one term and thought it very useful. I'll be putting more materials up this Fall 05 as a result.' On the other hand, some doubts were expressed by faculty who made use of the service at its early stage: '… not easy to plan time before start of course to incorporate e-reserves when viable alternatives exist' or 'I would prefer to give the students the citation and have them go and search for the article. This will develop researching skills. However, the constant changing of databases so that I can't get the articles is really frustrating.' Some faculty members mentioned alternatives to reserve services – 'availability of material which is in the public domain or available directly to students through e-journals' and 'course readers may cost more … but readers guarantee that students have access to all of the assigned texts for my course …'

It was obvious from the survey results that clarification and promotion of E-Reserve service had to be done, whether these were issues relating to the content of E-Reserve, the copyright constraints, the time needed for processing, or the benefits of Blackboard access over the library catalogue. In subsequent years, promotion to faculty was done through emails on faculty listservs at the beginning of terms, and at faculty workshops. There were some noticeable changes in E-Reserve demand, partly the result of increased Blackboard adoption by faculty over the years. The number of Blackboard E-Reserve links has grown from 474 in 2004/5, when E-Reserve was launched, to about 1,002 in the year 2007/8. The number of students enrolled in courses embedded with E-Reserve materials jumped from 1,969 students in 28 courses (2005/6) to 7,273 students in 79 courses (2007/8).

Nevertheless, there was very little that E-Reserve could do to address faculty desire for entire books assigned as course readings, except to suggest Print Reserve or course packs as more viable alternatives. There was a high demand for putting aside entire books, copies of book chapters or physical audio visual materials (VHS, DVD) on Print Reserve. The latter came as no surprise, as the Waterloo faculty survey in 2002 indicated the same desired formats. A rather surprising observation was that the demand for books on Print Reserve was similar for undergraduate and graduate programs. Ryerson University has developed rapidly in recent years from a mainly undergraduate university to a comprehensive university with approximately 25,000 undergraduate and graduate students (as of fall 2009), including 2,000 master's and PhD students. One would have thought that graduate programs were less dependent on prescribed readings but in reality, the demands for Print Reserve remained strong. From a separate analysis of faculty requests in the two years after E-Reserve was introduced in late 2004 (Appendix III), it was found that E-Reserve constituted 33–35% of Reserve requests submitted. Book requests remained much the same as before (52% in year 2003, 44% in 2004 and 54% in the months of January to April, 2005). However, reprints of articles or book chapters have gone down from 48% in 2003 (before E-Reserve was introduced) to 21% in 2004 (when E-Reserve was launched) and further down to 13% in 2005 (second year of E-Reserve operation).

The first student survey undertaken by Ryerson University's E-Reserve was very small-scale. It was a last-minute decision to survey students, within their Blackboard courses, at the end of the spring term in 2006 (Appendix IV). With faculty permission, a questionnaire was incorporated in four Blackboard courses. Twenty-two students completed the questionnaire. The survey was intended to be brief and focused on the main areas of interest to E-Reserve development at that stage: (1) remote vs. on-campus electronic access; (2) ease of access and frequency of problems; and (3) preferences of access. An overwhelming majority of 77% accessed e-reserve materials in Blackboard from home computers and 54% from work computers. Only 9% accessed the materials from library computers. Over 54% had problems accessing the full-text 1–5 times, while 45% never had any problems. When asked to compare their preference for print course packs sold at the bookstore or short-term loans checked out from the library's Circulation Desk, an even greater majority of 90% supported links to electronic materials posted on E-Reserve within Blackboard courses.

Ryerson's E-Reserve recognized right from the start of its pilot project that the Distance Education (DE) department would be the biggest user. The pilot project was directed at DE. It was only natural that a larger-scale student survey was planned with DE students in mind. Instead of creating a separate E-Reserve survey, attempts were made in 2007 to integrate E-Reserve questions into the DE Department's regular end-of-term student surveys (Appendix V). Two such surveys were carried out in March and November of 2007. The March survey had 863 respondents and the November survey had 833 respondents. Again, E-Reserve questions were intended to be short, as they formed only part of a much longer survey administered by the DE Department. The questions were also designed to fit in with the style of the general DE survey.

Like the previous student mini-survey undertaken in 2006 (Appendix IV), the theme continued to be ease and speed of accessing links, as saving students' time in conducting research was considered the top criterion for measuring effectiveness of library service. Both surveys indicated that students did not have much trouble seeing full text of an article on E-Reserve. Twenty-two per cent of those surveyed in March 2007 never had any problems seeing full text of an article and 28% in the November survey found it easy to locate online readings within the Blackboard course home page. Only 1% in the March survey had problems 6–10 times and 9% in the latter survey did not find it easy to locate E-Reserve readings. Answers to questions on viewing streaming videos or opening up an article link or seeing a full-text article showed a similar range of percentages. Complaints were more often in the open-ended question section. Not having a single sign-on to library resources within Blackboard was a known source of frustration. This was a much bigger issue that required the attention of the library and the university. The implementation of the EZproxy process in 2008 has removed the extra step of library authentication once a student logs into Blackboard, and addressed the main concern of E-Reserve access. Regarding direct links to full text articles, E-Reserve staff have exercised judgment in providing full text right away or presenting users with the SFX menu of multiple links to the same article. The matter was brought to the attention of the Digital Support Librarian, who is responsible for managing the library's local instance of the OCUL Scholars Portal SFX service. The Digital Support Librarian as part of the Scholars Portal Public Services Advisory Group, found at *http://spotdocs.scholarsportal.info/display/ PSWG*, engaged in an investigation to assess user attitude towards DirectLink and SFX. In the summer of 2009, 5 OCUL institutions surveyed their users on their perceptions of frequency of technical problems, ease of navigation, value of help options on SFX menus, and other features related to SFX. In general, perceptions of the SFX service proved to be more positive than the investigators had anticipated, but several comments confirm that there does exist some dissatisfaction with the number of steps, windows, and clicks needed to get from article citation to article full text. Some examples follow:

- 'When we click on it, we should automatically be sent to the article and not to another search engine where we have to retype the title in order to access it. It's a step that is a waste of time and frustrating.' – Undergraduate student, Business and Management.

- '... it would be nice to get the full article by just one click from "Get It! Ryerson".' – Academic staff, Engineering, Architecture and Science.

- 'For some articles there are multiple links available labeled "Full Text" and it took me a while to figure out that they were all the same, just hosted on different servers, some more reliable than others. It's not very clear what to do when so many links are available.' – Graduate student, Business and Management.

- 'It's a bit of a hassle. Have to go through it instead of directly accessing journal articles.' – Undergraduate student, Community Services.

While the two issues described above were either influenced by external changes or technical constraints, students' lack of awareness of the E-Reserve service reflected badly on Ryerson E-Reserve's publicity and user education efforts. In both DE surveys, nearly half of the students did not use the service or were not aware of it. In the March 2007 survey, 59% and 78% answered 'not applicable' to the two questions on problems seeing full text or viewing streaming videos on E-Reserve. In the November 2007 survey, 61% replied 'never used E-Reserve' to the questions on ease of locating online readings and 55% to opening up links to full text documents. Several answers to the open-ended question indicated inadequate understanding of what E-Reserve really was. There were general remarks about looking up the library's electronic resources, the complications of searching databases, and the time involved in getting relevant results. The examples given were more related to searching library articles and indexes, rather than E-Reserve readings. A few students asked for online tutorials, videos or other means to help them navigate the screens. Students' lack of awareness also reflected on faculty's knowledge or adoption of the service. As one student put it, 'All online courses should have the readings on E-Reserve.' Ryerson University currently has about 1,800 online courses, of which Continuing Education, including Distance Education, has at least 200–300 online courses. The Library E-Reserve statistics indicated a surge in faculty requests since 2004, but the figures did not include the number of courses where faculty posted links to documents themselves on their own course pages, bypassing the Library, and Blackboard – the University's learning portal. There is no doubt that more promotion should be done to encourage faculty to make their readings available electronically in Blackboard. A different strategy may be necessary, besides the use of the DE Faculty Handbook, DE's Online Community pages, the faculty listserv and library Web pages. Alongside the promotional efforts, there should also be an assessment of the impact on staff workload so that E-Reserve does not fall victim to its own success. The increase in faculty requests had put so much pressure on the one staff member who did the processing and copyright clearance that extra staff assistance was requested during peak periods. The E-Reserve librarian and staff are examining commercial systems such as ERes and Ares and assessing how they may be adapted to suit local needs.

Seize the opportunity whenever it appears

From library catalogue to Blackboard access

A snapshot of changes that happened to the e-reserve operation in Ryerson University Library demonstrates the need to adapt to local demands and circumstances. Ryerson University Library started its e-reserve project in 2004 with provision of access via the library catalogue (Innovative Interfaces). Within months, E-Reserve embarked on a pilot project to launch the e-reserve module in the Blackboard Course Management System. Part of the incentive came from the Digital Media Projects Office (DMP), a unit of the Computing and Communication Services (CCS) charged with the responsibility of supporting teaching and learning technology and development. They wanted to experiment with that module within Blackboard and invited the library to participate.

Cheung and Patrick (2007) described the pros and cons of this collaboration. The library catalogue's proxy server was able to prevent non-Ryerson users from accessing copyrighted content through the library authentication process at that time (library barcode and PIN). Blackboard, however, offered the controlled access to materials by specific course, a requirement by publishers for copyright reasons. Students' convenience was a consideration. For courses that were delivered through Blackboard, students would not have to exit Blackboard to retrieve e-reserve readings from the library catalogue. The project would set the stage for the library's entry into the university's mainstream computing environment, and enable E-Reserve to be a partner in the portal development to support e-learning. DMP would help to promote the E-Reserve service to students and faculty, and provide the technical support and server space for this initiative. E-Reserve was fast in accepting this offer of collaboration. DMP helped in identifying faculty testers to launch the E-Reserve module in Blackboard's Content System. Faculty were advised to give the library's E-Reserve staff course builder access to their course shells so that library-created links could be uploaded in their course folders. The granting of course builder permission encountered very little resistance. The privacy issue is something which the Ryerson E-Reserve staff discovered, over the months and years following, to be a hard nut to crack at many other institutions in the province, and even in the country.

Moving from persistent links to OpenURL

Yet a few months later in May 2005, Ryerson's E-Reserve took on another pilot project – the use of OpenURL links vs. persistent links for bringing up the assigned electronic readings within Blackboard. Almost none of the Ontario libraries surveyed by email at that time was interested in, or had considered this approach. One e-reserve manager was quoted as saying '… this is counter to the principle of e-reserve'. However, Ryerson's E-Reserve staff were interested in taking advantage of the SFX link resolver to offer users a menu of choices of connections to the same article, stability sometimes lacking in the direct-link-to-one-article method. The library has no control over publishers' merging, acquisition activities or aggregator licensing agreements with publishers. 'When links suddenly became broken and only citations/abstracts remained, users had no idea what it meant except to blame the library for "frequently changing the databases," as one faculty put it' (Cheung & Patrick, 2007: 133).

SFX links were maintained centrally by the Collections Team of the library. SFX was implemented by academic libraries in the OCUL consortium and has been a service managed by the Scholars Portal Project since 2004. It was an opportunity for Ryerson's E-Reserve to make creative use of an existing technology. Library branding was another consideration. Students would recognize from the Get it! @ Ryerson menu that the links to articles were library resources and not Web materials freely accessible from anywhere on the Internet. The multiple access facility also had the advantage of giving users alternatives to access, when a particular link did not work. The citation seen by the users had more details than the library catalogue's brief bibliographic data. Furthermore, E-Reserve maintained that the screen with multiple choices of databases was the same as the one seen by users when they searched for articles and databases on the library Web page. Nothing was strange to the users. E-Reserve could have followed the footsteps of many of its predecessors to scan the articles for direct links to them, or select a particular database and copy the persistent link to that article. Ryerson E-Reserve staff chose to adopt both approaches, depending on the relative ease of creation of links to specific articles.

Working with copyright

Ryerson E-Reserve discovered that the Distance Education (DE) department had been streaming videos in some of their courses. They approached the library to assist with copyright clearance for videos in the library collection. Hence, in its second year of operation, Ryerson's E-Reserve found itself changing direction, taking on a new shape not envisaged in its original business plan for a start-up pilot.

Ryerson Library recognized the importance of copyright to the e-reserve process and from the start created a library lead hand position to manage copyright permissions. The process was entirely new to the library at that time, as the library was not involved at all with copyright clearance for the traditional print reserve materials. It has always been the faculty's responsibility to make sure that the materials they put on Print Reserve were copyright compliant. Neither was the library involved in preparing the print course packs sold at the university's bookstore. There are other copyright stakeholder groups on campus, including the Bookstore (compiling print course packs); Distance Education (leading provider of university-based adult learning and online distance education); the Office of Research Services (Ryerson's central research administration office and point of contact for financial support for university scholarly, research and creative activities); the Learning and Teaching Office (support and provide resources to faculty in their teaching); and the Digital Media Projects Office (assistance in the production and use of multimedia technologies for teaching and learning, including Ryerson's Blackboard learning system). However, there was no central coordinating office to deal with the copyright permission process or offer advice on copyright issues. As a result of E-Reserve's involvement in the copyright permission process, a Copyright Committee, consisting of librarians and staff from various library services, was formed in the library in June 2004, and an email account *copyrite@ryerson.ca* was introduced on the revamped library's copyright Website to answer questions on copyright issues related to library services. The Library's E-Reserve Librarian and Copyright Lead Hand were approached with copyright questions that were often beyond the scope of library services. Joint workshops with DMP, providing general guidelines on digital copyright, were offered to faculty and staff. In 2009, a copyright lawyer was invited to speak mainly to library staff, but the session was attended by several faculty members and administrative personnel. There was so much interest expressed in the subject that another copyright session would be planned for faculty and graduate students later in the year. A significant outcome of the electronic reserve development was the leadership role that the Library's E-Reserve took to educate the university community about copyright awareness.

Working with Distance Education and the Digital Media Projects Office

Within a short period of five years since its inception in 2004, Ryerson Library's E-Reserve has become a popular venue for faculty to integrate electronic reading materials in their courses, has established close working relationship with DE and the DMP, and has taken on a leading position in copyright related matters. The library had tried for many years in the past to work closely with other departments to deliver service in the common interest of serving the teaching, learning and research needs of the Ryerson community. Recognizing the large population of DE students at Ryerson University, the library placed emphasis on DE support by incorporating such responsibilities into one librarian position in the 1990s. The extent of support was limited to delivering physical materials to students in remote locations, on a case-by-case basis, and at the discretion of the librarian. There was little interaction with the DE course designers or the DE instructors regarding their development of course materials. The working relationship with the Computing and Communication Services department was also limited to server support for library resources (since the 1980s) or employment of student advisors in the recently created Information Commons (in the 2000s). Working so closely with DMP staff to support faculty in developing course materials in Blackboard was a significant change in the pattern of collaboration.

Look for new opportunities

The RefShare added value

Taking a proactive stance in growing beyond traditional boundaries is a key to survival or expansion in service. While Ryerson E-Reserve has established itself quite firmly as one of the faculty's and DE's chosen ways of creating and maintaining online reading lists, E-Reserve has been looking for ways to add value to materials delivered in this context. After almost five years of operation, Ryerson's E-Reserve is contemplating another change – this time, persuading faculty to create their own reading lists using RefShare. Apart from automatic linking through the integration between SFX and RefWorks, faculty can offer students the added value of creating proper bibliographies and interacting with the instructor when necessary.

Promotion of RefShare and E-Reserve was undertaken in 2007/2008. The first marketing effort was emailing the School of Nursing faculty in November 2007 since they were the top E-Reserve users and some of them RefWorks users as well. Another blanket email was sent in October 2008 on three university listservs (Research, Teaching and Faculty) to compare traditional e-reserve and the new RefShare method. A follow-up was made in the same month with the Lunch and Learn workshop session hosted by the DMP. Despite these efforts, there has been little response to date from faculty to try the new method. On the other hand, faculty's interest in using RefWorks for research and promoting it to their students has increased considerably since its promotion a couple of years ago. The RefWorks success is a combination of the efforts of subject librarians in promoting RefWorks in their research guides, in class instruction and general drop-in workshops. To persuade the faculty to take one further step in sharing their research results with students using RefShare may need more clarification of the relationship between traditional e-reserve done by staff and the benefits of RefShare, and marketing to targeted individuals.

Increasing audio visual content

Ryerson E-Reserve has striven to include more than textual reading materials for online delivery. It has provided support to Distance Education in clearing copyright for library owned videos. A further step it took was to increase its link to the multimedia databases acquired by the library. This is in keeping with the library's trend in recent years to invest a major part of its acquisition budget in online resources. Audio visual databases such as *Naxos Music Library*, Alexander Street Press' *Smithsonian Global Sound*, *ArtSTOR* and *Theatre in Video* are some notable subscriptions. These databases offer the capability for users to create playlists or folders so that materials selected or downloaded can be shared with other users. This presents opportunities for faculty to create reading lists to share with students in their classes. The E-Reserve Librarian, who also took up the responsibility of Audio Visual Services in 2007, was interested in promoting these resources and the playlists capabilities to faculty to form part of E-Reserve.

Enhance library integration with course management systems

Academic libraries have tried to integrate electronic reading lists or e-reserve materials within the parent institutions' course management system or the students' virtual learning environment. However, there does not appear to be a single path to achieve such integration. Local institutional culture, technical infrastructure and the extent of on-going technical support are essential components of any integration projects. The authors suspect that the conclusion reached by the CAUL study in Australia (Poleykett, 2003) probably holds true for other parts of the world. There is no best practice for e-reserve operation as its effectiveness is dependent on a lot of interaction with other administrative units inside and outside the library.

Various libraries have created workarounds to integrate library resources into the course management system. In response to the author's question posted on the Canadian Blackboard User Group Discussion List (*CAN-BUG@LISTS.BLACKBOARD.COM*) on December 5, 2008, one library described how it set up a Faculty Resources community space that allowed faculty or course designers access to a variety of resources, which they could then export to their Continuing Education course space. The library has created various course-related resources such as subject guides or searchable resources for the department, as well as a search box for locating these materials. Faculty copied and pasted the script into a header or footer on any page inside their course space so that students did not need to leave their course space to search library resources. Another librarian recommended developing a Folder or Learning Module of library resources and inserting the content into the template(s) created by each faculty or department when creating a new course. The librarian mentioned a significant pushback from students over outsiders having access to the class. A workaround proposed was to state upfront in the syllabus or other core course document about the service aspect of library access.

In another institution, there was a strong feeling that others should not have access to course assignments, discussion postings and quizzes. As well as instructors or course developers, Ryerson University Library was given course builder access to faculty course shells when helping them to create e-reserve links to documents. However, e-reserve counterparts in the University of Toronto or Seneca College in the same province were not given similar access to uploading documents in Blackboard.

Outside of Canada, Ohio State University in the United States started a pilot project, which they named as toolkit approach, to integrate library resources into the Desire2Learn learning management system (Black, 2008). E-reserve was the first tool of the toolkit. E-reserve staff made use of the Learning Object Repository in the course management system for storing e-reserve files. Key staff had the power to facilitate the placement of documents inside course shells and the power to turn on the course for users' access, hence delivering e-reserve materials to the course management system. This was followed by access to subscribed resources from links within the LMS, the creation of a special role for librarians within the LMS, and lastly, a library resource page within the LMS. The university specifically labeled the role as *librarians* to emphasize the collaboration between librarians and instructors in the teaching process and at the course specific level. However, as the Ryerson Library experience illustrated, not every institution or faculty member is in agreement with this concept. Privacy issues are obstacles to this team relationship. Librarians will have to feel their way around for an opportunity within the variety of options available for library presence in the virtual learning environment. An auto-population of library resources into the course management system, not involving any faculty permission and yet saving faculty time in organizing links in their course pages, provides a good beginning to the customization of library content to suit course needs. Gaining the trust and support of faculty to agree to the librarian access similar to a teaching assistant or course builder becomes the next step to realizing the goal of partnering with faculty to enhance the students' learning experiences. E-reserve is usually the first entry into the course management system or virtual learning environment. Information literacy is the next desirable collaboration. Information on new books and library materials, RSS feeds and other alerts to relevant resources, timely responses to students' concerns noted from the discussion boards in the CMS or VLE, and library quizzes and assignments are just some of the various methods that librarians can utilize to promote current awareness and critical thinking.

There is no best way or best timing as to how and when libraries can achieve the goals described above. Ryerson E-Reserve in Blackboard was started in 2004/5 and the library encountered no problems with getting course builder access to instructors' course shells. The dummy student account, created mainly for staff to provide help to students on searching their e-reserve materials, provides access to almost everything, except the grade book, in Blackboard. In reality, library staff seldom go beyond e-reserve to explore other features on the menu. A macro-level library tab within Blackboard, providing a link to the library home page, was inserted in 2007. However, it was not until early 2009 that a pilot project was proposed to auto-populate discipline-specific library resources into course shells. A catalyst in spurring on this project was the Distance Education department's interest in building course pages with relevant library subject resources. The timely formation of the library's Distance Education Committee to review current practices and offer service improvements brought in the necessary expertise from around the library (Web development, systems, collections, information literacy and e-reserve) to assess the desirability and feasibility of such an initiative. A further meeting with the DE and CCS confirmed the departmental needs, the willingness to collaborate and the technical issues involved. The immediate task for the project was to create a library database of the resources, appropriately coded and categorized so that these could be transferred to the corresponding coded course shells. Information about subject librarians, resources by subject and database descriptions had been scattered within the library's Website on separate HTML pages. To build the subject course shells, the choice was to either create a database using something like MySQL or build upon the existing ERM module (Electronic Resources Management) within the integrated library system (Millennium from Innovative Interfaces). The decision was to create a database, and solicit subject librarians' support to review their materials, and to assign course codes to the items. The library programmer set up the infrastructure while the university's CCS Department created the building block to Blackboard. The next hurdle will be adding librarians to Blackboard courses as *teaching assistants*. With such permission in Blackboard, librarians will have access to almost everything except the grading system.

Turn competition into partnership

Ryerson Library's E-Reserve has faced competition from other areas. One of the best strategies to deal with keen competition is to analyze the components of respective services, find out what are common among all, the comparative strengths and weaknesses, and look for ways to collaborate. This is a win-win strategy that benefits not only all participating parties, but most of all, the end-users.

Interaction with Distance Education

The co-operation of Ryerson University Library with the Digital Media Projects Office (DMP) in offering E-Reserve via the Content System in Blackboard has been described in detail in Chapter 3. The expanded working relationship with Distance Education (DE) course developers and designers is another by-product of E-Reserve operations. The DE department has its own technical support staff, resources, course development profiles and strategies. They maintain their own servers that are separate from the centralized system maintained by the university's Computing and Communication Services (of which the DMP is a part). Faculty requests from the department are channeled through the course developers. Expired E-Reserve files are removed by the department, as they control access to their own server. Their programmers have developed databases that store images and other digital learning objects created by their faculty or subscribed to by the department. They have their own copyright staff to seek permissions from rights holders to videos or documents not belonging to the library.

What brought them to the library then? Copyright was a common reason. DE realized that some of the articles needed for courses could be obtained through the library's database subscriptions, hence at no further cost to them. They knew that the library had a small e-reserve copyright budget to support expenses outside of the library subscriptions. When E-Reserve first started in 2004, the target users were DE students because their courses were mostly offered online and to off-campus students, sometimes in remote locations. The first test course was one that involved 29 readings from book chapters which, in the past, were assembled into a print course pack sold at the university's bookstore. Not surprisingly, the test did not go through, as the total cost amounted to more than CA$3,000, which neither the library nor DE were prepared to pay. There was some discussion on proposing an ancillary student fee to subsidize the cost the following year. However, the plan did not go through, as it was a very complicated issue to charge students extra for course materials, when there might be alternatives that could be used. At any rate, the common difficulty of dealing with copyright cost has brought the library and DE together to converse over guidelines, procedures, and even a shared database that would allow constituents (library staff, DE staff, DE faculty) to locate at any time the status of a copyright permission request and information on an approved or rejected case so that efforts would not be duplicated in locating publisher details. The database has not materialized as programming staff on both sides were too busy with other priorities to be able to focus on this undertaking. Nevertheless, there was recognition of common interest and a mutual desire to supplement or complement each other's efforts.

Ryerson Library is not alone in recognizing the benefits of partnership with DE. Jacksonville State University in the United States is another good example (Poe & McAbee, 2008). The DE Librarian worked closely with the Office of Distance Education (ODE). She sat on the Distance Education Advisory Committee and attended ODE staff meetings and workshops. Her close association with the ODE has enabled the library to maintain a presence in Blackboard, including the addition of a button or link to the library in the navigation panel in all Blackboard course shells. Although they have not achieved control of the tabs at the course level, the library link represents a significant step in the right direction of integrating library resources with the students' learning portal.

Interaction with IT support

The information technology (IT) department of an academic institution usually has a much larger pool of computing expertise than the library and it oversees hardware, software and server maintenance. Ryerson University's Computing and Communication Services (CCS), which encompasses the Digital Media Projects Office, also administers Blackboard, controlling the functioning of the Blackboard course management system, including the e-reserves module. The DMP personnel have been providing support to the library's E-Reserve operations through overall training of faculty in the use of the system, assistance in designing the e-reserve interface with the CMS and advice on Blackboard access issues in general. It cannot, however, fully comprehend the E-Reserve process outside of the system or monitor closely its efficiency. A big concern arising from Ryerson's E-Reserve's increased popularity is speed. Everything seemed to be slow from starting the e-reserve screen in Blackboard to posting links or uploading files to E-Reserve. When the issue was raised at a provincial e-reserve forum, other Blackboard participants at the meeting did not express a similar concern with their systems. To zero in on what appeared to be Ryerson's specific system environment, the library's System Librarian called for a joint meeting in June 2009 of all stakeholders – library system and E-Reserve personnel, and CCS's front and backend staff, including their manager. It was a much bigger meeting than the one the E-Reserve librarian had convened a year before. The meeting was very productive, generating various suggestions for cleaning up old files that were suspected of blocking the traffic. As well as storage for a large number of old courses whose materials were not being used, repeating the content of different sections of the same course had added to the load of the E-Reserve account. The recommendation was to add content to one course shell only and then link to this folder from other similar courses. A short-term project was for the library to identify courses they no longer needed access to, so that the university's Blackboard administrator could remove the E-Reserve account from these courses. This would involve checking with the instructors to determine whether content was still needed. A long term project was to remove the E-Reserve account from the disabled courses. The library technician could, at her discretion, remove the old course folder from the E-Reserve display or copy/move the existing content to a new course folder. A test account would be used to monitor the course removal and folder clean up within the E-Reserve account. The Blackboard administrator would also check the new Blackboard release for any changes in e-reserve protocol. All this may sound like simple housekeeping routines but a number of issues were considered, including the potential look-up and re-use of materials for future courses. What this incident demonstrated was the importance of cross-departmental collaboration and the involvement of all levels of staff from relevant areas. E-Reserve came to realize that it should not jump to the conclusion that the Blackboard system was at fault, without first diagnosing the environment within which the system was operating. E-Reserve could not rely solely on its own perception and explanation of problems without consulting other similar operations or system expertise beyond the library.

The streaming initiative

Another Ryerson E-Reserve initiative is video streaming, an area that is of interest to a wide array of services within the institution. In September 2008, E-Reserve called for a brainstorming session of all parties on campus involved in streaming initiatives. The meeting was attended by the library's own systems personnel, Special Collections Librarian, Institutional Repository Librarian, E-Reserve and Audio Visual Librarian and staff, DE Manager and the Assistant Director, and managerial and staff representatives from the CCS department. Apparently, each area had been involved in some aspects of video streaming but had not come together to hash out goals, constraints, requirements and future strategy. Audio Visual Services in the library has been reviewing its collection to identify more heavily used VHS to either purchase DVD replacements or consider the streaming options with distributors. The urgency of VHS replacement stemmed mainly from the impending withdrawal of VHS equipment support for smart classroom showings on campus, currently handled by the Media Services division of CCS. Special Collections is a new library department and the Institutional Repository is an even newer development. Both have an interest in digitization projects. DE wanted to make sure that any centralized streaming initiative would recognize their local need of extracting content from a variety of sources to compile their own course content for streaming on their local media server. The Rogers Communications Centre (a multi-media facility which serves the university's programs in media and electronic communications) brought attention to the demands on the institution's technical infrastructure, the compatibility and support of different streaming formats such as Windows Media Player and Flash, and the staff expertise required. The existing streaming support (bandwidth and staff resources) was designed more for live Webcasting of events rather than massive digitization projects for subsequent streaming. The DMP was part of an institution-wide iTunes and podcasting project. The meeting was a mere starting point for amalgamating the interests of various stakeholders. Nothing substantial was planned for the next step of co-operation but the very fact that the library was instrumental in getting these groups together in one room was a great step forward. Another set of silos had been broken down. Participation in this meeting signaled to all parties concerned that streaming is more than a localized and exclusive project but has the potential for further co-operation and collaboration in future.

Digital course packs and digital textbooks

Digital textbooks are slowly making their way into the textbook industry, and could account for as much as 15% of university textbook sales in North America by 2011/2012 (Pritchard, 2009). CourseSmart, a U.S.-based company, offers more than 7,000 university and college textbooks for courses in Canada and the U.S., while Flat World Knowledge has published textbooks being used in 400 college classrooms (Valentine, 2009). Not only are the textbooks, together with diagrams, charts and graphics, downloadable onto laptops but also to smart phones or onto thin and light-weight reading devices, like Amazon.com's Kindle or Sony's Reader. While the acquisition of digital texts may reduce the cost of textbook purchases by nearly 50% to 60%, as the publishers said, the majority of students still hang on to the printed version, and try to recover expenses by selling their used books at the end of the term. A major deterrent to digital textbook acquisition is the cost model. Digital purchases are often subscription-based and ownership expires after a defined period of time. Students will not be able to review the materials later on, when they need to do so. CourseSmart offers e-textbooks for about half the cost of the print version. After purchase, the digital textbooks are available for 180 days (Cox, 2009). There are some free textbook models but availability of content is more limited.

Nonetheless, the reduced cost, the searching flexibility not available with physical text, the interactive component in some digital versions, and mobility of access may eventually change the learning landscape. Instructors will not need to request for an entire textbook or photocopies of textbooks to be put on the library's print reserve. Digital textbooks may become an attractive alternative to library e-reserve, as well as other options such as purchasing PDF files and audio versions of text materials.

There have been some positive outcomes from partnerships between publishers and universities. At the University of Kansas in the United States (Burich & Rholes, 2004), faculty were directly approached by XanEdu, a product of ProQuest, for the creation of digital course packs sold to students but initially with no library development. As expected, a lot of the journal article content in these course packs was from the ProQuest databases, which the library subscribed to. Students were charged unnecessarily for these copyright costs on the course pack content. The university's solution was to have an agreement with the company whereby library staff would check the faculty document selections against the library holdings before incorporating them in the course packs. Materials owned by the library or those that could be claimed as fair use would be included free of charge. It was a labor-intensive process. However, by doing so, the university would not be double charged for providing access to the same content. Students, too, would not have to pay higher fees for course packs arising from unnecessary copyright costs.

Embrace a new culture that is user-centered and work towards service convergence

The OCLC E-Learning Task Force (2003) presented a report on *Libraries and the enhancement of e-learning*, and provided some insightful recommendations. First, the report emphasized that the academic world has moved towards student-centered services instead of a teacher-centric model. Secondly, libraries had to recognize that they may not necessarily own the materials needed by students, or the resources they were helping to manage or provide access to. Thirdly, librarians and staff had to be equipped with a new set of skills that would enable them to support the students' new learning behavior. Fourthly, students' preference was to learn within one single Web space, where they could search for information, organize it in their own way and share with peers, communicate with their instructors and obtain grading for their assignments, as well as creating their own e-portfolios to organize and track their work. In most cases, this is learning within a course or learning management system environment.

To develop a sustainable, coherent and seamless infrastructure in support of this learning behavior, the Task Force recommended collaboration of all stakeholders within the institution (the faculty, the library, IT and the instructional design department). Two main collaborative opportunities were identified by the Task Force between the library and its academic partners: (1) integrating existing and new library and institutional services into the e-learning infrastructure; and (2) managing digital asset repositories. The Task Force was probably right to say that very few institutions had achieved either objective. Among the obstacles identified were lack of a common language on which to build these strategic initiatives and the existence of cultural barriers, including resistance to change and maintaining one's own distinctive view. A notable example of inconsistent partnership mentioned in the OCLC Report was digital initiatives, which almost every campus group had vested interest in, but seldom involved all major stakeholders. There was a lack of vision to rise above traditional organizational boundaries to work towards a common service model that placed emphasis on ease and convenient access from the student perspective. 'The real problem though' as the Task Force concluded, 'is not necessarily organizational convergence but service convergence' (OCLC, 2003: 8).

In an article on Institutional Repositories, the importance of collaboration among stakeholders for building and maintaining this essential infrastructure for scholarship in the digital age was emphasized.

While operational responsibility for these services may reasonably be situated in different organizational units at different universities, an effective institutional repository of necessity represents a collaboration among librarians, information technologists, archives and records managers, faculty, and university administrators and policymakers. (Lynch, 2003, 'Defining Institutional Repositories', para. 1)

Another study that examined the nature and value of undergraduate students' experiences with the academic library also emphasized the importance of collaboration (Kuh & Gonyea, 2003). The data represented responses from more than 300,000 students between 1984 and 2002 to the College Student Experiences Questionnaire. The findings of this study indicated that to produce an information-literate college graduate, the campus as a whole should act together in promoting the value of information literacy on and off campus, as well as providing students with the opportunity to evaluate the quality of information encountered. Librarians were asked to redouble their efforts to collaborate with faculty members, instructional development staff, and student affairs professionals in creating such opportunities for students.

A library literature search revealed some institutional collaborative efforts towards the e-learning infrastructure based upon the course management system or the students' virtual learning environment. In some cases, the management of digital asset repositories was a collaborative venture between the library and faculty and some other academic partners. In Chapter 2 under 'Repository-based approach', the project of the University of Western Australia Library was an example of a centralized, institution-wide electronic repository of teaching and learning materials to 'implement a course related materials management system that facilitates the online teaching and learning activities of the University' (Poleykett & Benn, 2003: 3). The Management and Steering Committees members were drawn from across the university, including representatives from the University Chancellery, Student Services, the Legal Services Office, the Student Guild, Faculties, and the Library, which were all stakeholders in the centralized repository project. The university also investigated the practicalities of using the repository to store other learning materials, not necessarily library-related and separate from the proprietary LMS. Chapter 5 described a library streaming project at Coventry University in England (Gibbs, 2009). The term e-reserve is not used but the videos were course-specific and have been linked through the OPAC, the university's VLE (virtual learning environment) and the Equella digital repository software.

The streaming project was a collaborative effort by the library's Media Services, the university's IT services, and the e-Learning Unit. The latter was formed in 2007 by the university with the mission of supporting the institutional VLE, which included e-learning tools and objects, and an institutional repository was created.

On the other hand, there were also examples illustrating how difficult it was to achieve such a shared vision. Chapter 6 described the difficulties of libraries trying to integrate e-reserve materials within the institutions' course management system. Some libraries in Canada were not given course builder access to faculty course shells within Blackboard. Ryerson University E-Reserve has such access to assist faculty with e-reserve readings but wanted to go one step beyond to partner with faculty in creating and integrating course-specific library resources into the course pages. Security and privacy concerns were raised by the IT department. Little progress has been made since a librarian submitted a position paper, arguing for the importance of this service convergence with faculty to provide students with the ease and convenience of searching information and obtaining help at the point of need. The Ryerson E-Reserve Librarian posted a question on this subject to the Canadian Blackboard listserv. One librarian remarked that even the students may be resistant towards having a third party – the librarians – involved in their virtual learning environment, besides themselves and their instructors.

Nevertheless, whether the library's entry point into the users' learning space is via the courseware environment or through a popular search engine or archival digital collections outside the library, it is true that users will expect seamless access to these resources and services anywhere, anytime. The ARL Report (Association of Research Libraries, 2009) portrayed a shift away from localization of content and services to a deeper integration of access to resources and services through a wide array of entry points, including the campus systems and the broader Web environment. It predicated that in the 2015 technology environment, local management and storage of digital content would be substituted by distribution and collaboration within the institution, across institutions or contracting out to the commercial sector. 'Interoperability' between systems would be the norm. 'Library-centric' standards would be taken over by the ability to apply Web-enabled 'external standards' (p. 32) to achieve that blending into a broader information environment that would be user-centric and service-oriented. To be part of this new digital culture, libraries, as the Association predicated, would need to 'cultivate and expose the "aggregate library resource" in order to gain greater visibility among many competing information alternatives' (p. 33). The report mentioned some examples of collaboration that have already emerged. These included the Massachusetts Institute of Technology's Open Courseware program in the United States that organized the dissemination of course materials using a publishing model; and Scholars Portal services, a cooperative service development in the Ontario Council of University Libraries (OCUL) in Canada. Scholars Portal services, as the ARL Report (2009: 25) explained,

> include preservation, and access management for a range of content types including: electronic Journals (13.3 million locally archived articles from 8,300 journals from 20 scholarly publishers); index and abstract databases (more than 200 with over 150 million citations); research repository works (housed in a number of instances of DSpace); electronic book collections will soon include scholarly e-books (30,000 contemporary titles and 160,000 out of copyright titles) and research data (a numerical, statistical, and geospatial information service will soon support a wide range of information resources and, where possible, integrate these resources with other services).

Be responsive to administrative change

As libraries adapt to both technological and legislative changes in the local environment, digitization projects have speedily gained momentum, and such development has also had an impact on e-reserve. Responding to a CAUL survey (Poleykett, 2003), the University of New South Wales described how a full service of digitized exam papers was put in place following the 2000 amendments to the Australia Copyright Act. In the years subsequent to copyright legislation changes, Reserve and Digitization were restructured as part of the Online Services Department, joining up with Library Web Coordination, the Australian Digital Theses Program and other initiatives as they arose. Ex Libris' DigiTool was implemented in the hope of better managing the entire mass of digital material, whether these were images, audio or video files or texts. Poleykett and Benn (2003) described how the implementation of their repository-based reading list management system at the University of Western Australia presented the library with the opportunity for reviewing the workflow and methods of delivery of course materials and examination papers on line, as well as the impetus to develop a new organizational model that impacted on the library and the university as a whole. A new Digital Repositories Unit was established within the Asset Management section of the library. This unit was responsible for the overall coordination of the service and staff training. The subject librarians' role was retained, but at a reduced level, in liaising with academic staff regarding issues on support, training and placing of items on physical reserve. As well as co-coordinating the management of course materials online and examination papers online, the unit would also be responsible for other digital collections, digital theses and repositories of other materials as the demand arose.

Within five years of its history, the E-Reserve operation in Ryerson University Library has undergone two administrative changes. The E-Reserve unit was set up in 2004, as part of the Borrower Services Team of the library, along with other partners, namely Circulation, Reserve, Stack Maintenance, Interlibrary Loan and Audio Visual. A Copyright Lead Hand position was created and hired at a level just below Library Technicians, the paraprofessionals who assist the professional librarians in performing a variety of functions, ranging from reference service to technical duties such as cataloguing, and interlibrary loan operations. The Lead Hand also had to work closely with the Print Reserve Lead Hand and took part in supervising the Circulation staff in front desk duties. The creation of the Special Collections and the Institutional Repository units in 2008/9 meant a re-shuffling of responsibilities among librarians. The Audio Visual Librarian took on the Special Collections portfolio. E-Reserve was combined with Audio Visual, partly because of the previous working experience of the E-Reserve librarian in Audio Visual Services, and partly because the E-Reserve Librarian advocated e-learning support that would include e-reserve, the booking or reserving of audio visual materials in the library collection and the lending of materials to other institutions, and also streaming of audio visual materials.

The concept was inspired by what evolved at the University of Guelph in Canada. In 2006, Guelph announced a new unit called E-Learning Operations and Reserve Services, which handled both the traditional print reserve services and supported the faculty in converting materials from print to online delivery, taking care of the technical process and the copyright permission procedures. In Asia, in 2007/8, the University of Hong Kong Libraries, who started e-reserve much earlier than Ryerson Library, announced a department of Audio Visual and Reserve. The latter operation includes print course packs as well as online course packs.

Ryerson's E-Reserve operation is constantly evolving and mutating in unexpected ways – integrating with the course management system, working along with RefShare and SFX and finding common ground with multimedia database delivery. The E-Reserve Librarian's role had to be flexible enough to take on new challenges, as the relationship with Distance Education became more pronounced through E-Reserve. The E-Reserve Librarian was formerly in charge of Audio Visual and Interlibrary Loan services. It was a matter of timing and administrative moves that brought ahead the amalgamation of E-Reserve, Audio Visual and Distance Education support under the leadership of one librarian – the E-Reserve Librarian. It was again timing that the Copyright Lead Hand resigned and the Library decided to turn that position into a generic Library Technician role so that there was more flexibility in managing staff resources across units. The staff member could enjoy more variety of experiences beyond processing e-reserve requests. The end result was an outcome that represented the active push of the e-learning ideal and an acceptance of a change in administrative priorities.

Hersey (2005) pointed out the many changes in e-reserve that make it a service less and less affiliated with the traditional Circulation and Reserve services. E-reserve has evolved from a service that was primarily scanning materials at faculty's requests, and staff are now inevitably involved in copyright considerations, determining if materials requested by faculty are available in full text, in the public domain, or whether fair use or fair dealing can be applied without seeking copyright permissions from either the copyright collectives or individual rights holders. These decisions may involve either direct contact or indirect liaison with other staff dealing with acquisition and obtaining streaming rights for audio or video clips. E-reserve access has gone beyond the realm of Circulation or even the library's OPAC to course management systems such as WebCT, Blackboard and Angel. In some libraries, e-reserve readings may derive from the institution's learning objects repository and are then imported into faculty's course pages. Hersey was of the opinion that what have been e-reserve functions can be incorporated into a 'Course Support Department,' providing faculty with the support they need in their teaching activities. Such teaching support could include assistance with linking or scanning full text documents to course pages, providing information on copyright, offering help on instructional technology, and informing faculty of bibliographic instruction opportunities available. Hersey referred to the results of a Web-based survey on usage of information and communication technologies by college professors at the University of Idaho in the United States for research and teaching (Jankowska, 2004). The faculty there would like to see more staff and better equipment in the interlibrary loan department and an expanded e-reserve with the addition of new audio visual formats. The findings from the two questions about the possibility of creating a faculty virtual center confirmed the belief that faculty wanted library support for their teaching activities. They needed help in finding information on distance learning courses and developing online classes and learning materials. Instead of staff taking on these functions as add-on responsibilities or participating in work groups or committees, the recommendation was to make the provision of such a service an integral part of staff duties. Library service would be more cost-effective in this way, and this new department would reinforce library efforts in outreach programs to faculty and distance education staff.

Take the lead in copyright literacy

According to the 2008 survey undertaken by Ryerson University librarians (Appendix I) and the CAUL report (Poleykett, 2003), universities do not always have a central copyright office or officer to handle campus copyright issues. There may be intellectual property offices to deal with authors' rights rather than those of users. E-reserve or the library often become the default unit for copyright administration. E-reserve services are most impacted by copyright permission charges and e-reserve staff have the most direct contact with faculty regarding copyright interpretations and payment issues. Libraries should take full advantage of this position to help promote education of copyright on campus and cooperate with other copyright stakeholders, internal and external, to achieve a balanced approach to the interpretation of copyright – asserting the users' rights while respecting those of the owners. In the same way that libraries are charged with the responsibility of coordinating information literacy programs for the institution as a whole, libraries should take a proactive approach in taking on the mission of promoting copyright literacy on campus.

What are some effective methods of promoting copyright literacy? Horava (2009) examined the copyright Web pages of Canadian libraries. Explanations of copyright legislation, licenses and terms of agreement signed with copyright collectives were taking the centre stage whereas explaining the impact of copyright on research and learning or integrating such content in the course management system were relegated to an inconspicuous spot. Advocacy of copyright reform was almost negligible. When libraries were asked to rate the effective methods of communicating copyright information on campus, first priority was given to faculty liaison and outreach, above the use of Web pages and individual assistance. The education component is the area that libraries identified as their biggest challenge, aside from interpretive (understanding the law, the limitations and permissions) and organizational (staff resources and coordination on campus) challenges. There were reports of widespread misunderstanding or inconsistencies in understanding of copyright and its restrictions or permissions. These misconceptions, as Horava noticed, were not limited to one particular user group. Developing a respect for copyright was even harder in these days, he said, where open access was regarded as the way to go for information resources. Users mistakenly think that, 'if something is free on the Web, it is "free" and can be "freely" used'.

There may not be a universal approach to handling copyright in libraries. However, there needs to be a consistent policy stating clearly what the limitations or permissions are for learning, teaching and scholarly communication. Designating an individual in the library to take the lead in coordinating copyright related activities and in promoting copyright awareness seems like a logical step. Ryerson University librarians have heard comments from faculty that they were not sure from whom in the library they could seek copyright assistance. When they had an audio visual copyright question, should they go to the AV Librarian? When they were uncertain about posting Web pages in their courses, should they ask the Blackboard administrator who helped them setting up course pages, the subject librarians or somebody in the library?

Be responsive to external forces of change

IMS and EDUCAUSE

The OCLC Task Force on E-Learning (2003) reported on IMS' initiative to reach out to the library communities and form a Digital Libraries Special Interest Group. IMS Global Learning Consortium, Inc. was originally entitled the Instructional Management Systems project, but the organization found the longer name to be confusing and prefers to be called IMS. IMS, found at *http://www.imsglobal.org/faqs/imsnewpage.cfm?number*, is a global, non-profit, member organization that works to facilitate the growth of learning technology in the education and corporate learning sectors. Forty-seven per cent of their member organizations have headquarters outside the United States. The Digital Libraries Special

Interest Group initiative and the White Paper produced in 2004 represented a departure for IMS in that it was 'specifically aimed at a community that has not been traditionally involved in IMS' (OCLC, 2003: 15).

The IMS White Paper (McLean & Lynch, 2004) illustrated the difference between the push and pull of information resources in the learning process. Learning activity was once regarded as static, with relatively little interaction between the activity itself and the information resources. Students had to logout of the course/learning management system (CMS/LMS) to look for e-reserve materials held in the library system. Instructors had to obtain external document links or scanned articles to post within the CMS/LMS. The format of information resources was also restricted to static text-based articles. The approach adopted was library-centric and the thinking was very much pushing information into the CMS/LMS. Increasingly, the library and the learning worlds have come to realize that the learners may not want to be restricted to third party commercialized information resources during their learning activity. They may want to pull any type of information – text, streamed audio/video, their own works, contributions of their peers or their instructors' lecture notes – into their research activity at the point of need. A new kind of thinking has led the library to go beyond integrating their existing resources and services, such as virtual reference, subject guides and article databases into the CMS/LMS, but into the importing and exporting of objects between the library and course/learning management systems. One example of such objects is e-reserve readings. The digital objects now include streamed audio or video, and not just text. To support this creative flow of information and activities between the library and e-learning systems, a new type of information architecture is needed. It is this necessity for a new service model that brought together the IMS and the library community. The IMS White Paper continued to describe a digital campus that combines the two concepts of digital information management and learning system management. It cited examples of contributions of the library community such as Z39.50 application, and the work of IMS around the concept of common services that support all types of applications and repositories, including e-learning and research knowledge repositories. The White Paper concluded that libraries should recognize that services may, or may not, be part of an integrated library any more. The focus of service development should be on service-oriented architectures, such as Web Services, that could involve a series of applications covering the OPACs, e-reserves, portals and document delivery services. The White Paper pointed out that many other industries outside the library were also focusing their attention on service-oriented technologies and infrastructures. Hence, both the library and learning management systems should be prepared to adopt institution-wide services instead of creating their own. The White Paper has formed the basis for wider consultation with library communities on their functional requirements in the e-learning space. Library communities, and e-reserve as a component, should keep on top of these developments and be responsive to the call for collaboration and consultation, as greater collaboration with all stakeholders in the e-learning environment, internal or external, is not only desirable, but essential.

As well as the IMS, there are other organizations that advance higher education by promoting the use of information technology. EDUCAUSE is another non-profit association with membership open to institutions of higher education, corporations serving the higher education information technology and other related organizations. The Educause Web site, found at *http://www.educause.edu/home*, boasts a membership of over 2,200 colleges, universities and education organizations, including 250 corporations. The Association of Research Libraries (ARL), found at *http:// www.arl.org/*, is a member of EDUCAUSE. Like IMS, EDUCAUSE is an organization not just for the IT and instructional design community but also for the library world. As libraries become more user-focused, service-oriented and technology-driven, it is important that they should go outside the library-centric mode of thinking and work along with other education technology service providers to create a common information and service architecture and infrastructure that support the new digital learning culture.

The new generation of faculty members

The changing demographics of academic library users, staff, and faculty members may affect how links to content are created. As more young and technologically-savvy faculty members are hired to fill retirements, self-sufficiency in creating links and setting up their own access to required readings is likely to increase. The libraries' role in facilitating e-reserves will be more focused on performing the behind-the-scenes technical work in building the collections and optimizing search and discovery tools.

Just as academic libraries have observed changes in their student population's behaviors and preferences towards learning in general, and technologies in particular, they may begin to see these changes among faculty as well. Digital Natives, Millennials, or the Net Generation, that much-discussed demographic group born between about 1980 and 1994 are in 2010 now, on the eldest side of the span, 29 years old. Though there has not been strong empirical evidence proving the extent of the differences between this generation and those that were born before them (Bennett, Maton & Kervin, 2008), the fact is that, especially in developed countries, most of this generation will have grown up with technology as part of their lives. Further, those born in or after 1994 will never have known a time without the Internet. The authors anticipate that new, incoming faculty members will be more comfortable building their own reading lists with little or no need to consult the library for technical assistance. As more newly degreed faculty members join university staff, they may also exchange knowledge and have an impact on their peers in terms of comfort level with IT. To benefit from these changes, the library may be able to point to instructions that can be used by faculty to generate persistent URLs or OpenURLs for subscribed library content. Faculty members may become more independently able to create their own reading lists with minimal documentation and occasional support.

Federated search and discovery layers

A major barrier to faculty and other non-library institutional units' ability to create online reading lists to subscribed resources is the wide variety of platforms represented in library databases and their corresponding differences in terms of obtaining persistent or durable links. The library would have to maintain some sort of instructions so that these outside units can create links that will work off campus as well as on campus for the duration of a given course. A set of instructions covering a multitude of databases may be intimidating and hinder these groups' feeling of confidence in creating their own links.

Products such as Serials Solutions' Summon, or Innovative Interfaces' Encore, that promise to enable a single search interface for library resources have the potential to significantly reduce the complexities involved in linking to library resources. If indeed librarians are able to provide a one-stop search and discovery and access to their collections, there should then be a corresponding one-stop linking procedure that can be used. As long as there is a single procedure, instructions can be created so that faculty, students, and staff can all link to available resources without extensive and convoluted steps and instructions.

It may also become possible with these tools to integrate with Course Management Systems so that the creation of lists is made seamless as with a drag-and-drop or similarly user-friendly method.

Open Access and Creative Commons

E-reserve over the years has grown beyond being an online equivalent of the traditional print reserve or a place for storing more heavily demanded materials for faster circulation. However, print reserve, especially copies of book chapters or the whole books themselves, has maintained its popularity. A lot of such stability is attributable to copyright restrictions. A whole book cannot be scanned and made accessible online, even if the users are willing to pay the hefty copyright permission costs. There is simply a limit on how much one can copy of the whole book. Despite the increased production of e-books, including some more current titles than previously available, the percentage of e-book content that faculty select for recommended readings is small compared with the hard copies. Ryerson Library's print reserve statistics confirm this phenomenon. The quantities of articles requests have dropped significantly but the number of physical book requests has gone even higher, probably in tandem with the increase of graduate level courses offered.

In the midst of the tug of war between users and providers of information, there emerges another force that advocates for and creates the environment for free exchange of information without the fear of copyright infringement – the open access publishing and Creative Commons. Suber (2004) defined Open Access (OA) literature as 'digital, online, free of charge, and free of most copyright and licensing restrictions. What makes it possible is the internet and the consent of the author or copyright-holder' (para. 1). He continued to say that:

> OA literature is not free to produce, even if it is less expensive to produce than conventionally published literature. The question is not whether scholarly literature can be made costless, but whether there are better ways to pay the bills than by charging readers and creating access barriers. Business models for paying the bills depend on how OA is delivered. (para. 4)

OA literature has grown significantly in recent years. Morrison (2009) provided in her blog some figures that illustrated the dramatic increase:

Directory of Open Access Journals (DOAJ)

- Over 4,000 fully open access, peer reviewed scholarly journals;
- adding two titles per day.

OpenDOAR (Directory of Open Access Repositories)
- About 1,500 open access repositories worldwide;
- adding one new repository every business day.

Scientific Commons
- 30 million scientific publications free online;
- added eight million publications in the last year;
- growing by more than 20,000 publications per day.

PubMedCentral
- 20% of world's medical literature freely available two years after publication;
- close to 10% of world's medical literature freely available immediately on publication;
- one new journal chooses to submit all or most content to PMC every business day;
- more medical journals become fully open access in PMC every other business day.

PLoS ONE
- If current trends continue, *PloS ONE*, published by the Public Library of Science, a non-profit publisher, will become the largest journal in 2010.

It was reported that 'more than two thirds of academic journals now permit self-archiving on author web sites or in institutional repositories, including all Elsevier journals' ('A shot heard', 2008).

The OA movement has gained support from the academic community. In February 2008, Harvard University's Faculty of Arts and Sciences approved a motion that requires Harvard researchers to deposit their scholarly articles in an OA repository to be managed within the library and to be made accessible freely on the Web ('A shot heard', 2008). Other universities in the United States are actively considering a similar policy. In an Open Letter released on 23 September 2009, 57 educational leaders of U.S. universities and colleges declared support of the Federal Research Public Access Act of 2009 (S.1373), aimed to ensure public access to publicly funded research in the U.S. ('57 College Presidents', 2009). The growing trend of OA is not limited to the United States. Neither do stakeholders consist of faculty only. Funding agencies in

Europe including the RCUK and the Wellcome Trust are supporting open access. Librarians are behind the movement as well. As mentioned by Stuart Shieber, the Harvard University professor of computer science who presented the historic open access mandate for approval by the University's Faculty of Arts and Sciences, librarians were very much involved at different stages of the process and the making of the policy at Harvard ('A shot heard', 2008).

Another development that impacts the publishing and copyright landscape is the emergence of Creative Commons (CC), found at *http:// creativecommons.org/*. Established in 2001, Creative Commons is a non-profit organization consisting of cyberlaw, intellectual property, academic and filmmaking professionals dedicated to making it easier for people to share, remix, use commercially and build upon the work of others, while respecting the legality of copyright. CC provides free licenses and other legal tools to mark creative work, giving creators the freedom to decide what the rights would entail. A notable example of the use of Creative Commons licenses is Flickr, found at *http://www.flickr.com/*, a social photo-sharing site where many users have allowed the reuse and remixing of their content through Creative Commons. In 2008, CC boasted an estimated 130 million licensed works. These works are considered items in the public domain that can be placed on reserve without consideration of fair use. Academic libraries in the United States, such as Montgomery College Libraries, found at *http://www.montgomerycollege.edu/library/ coursereserves_faculty.html*, have made references in their e-reserve guidelines and copyright information for faculty: 'Items in the public domain, those copyrighted before 1923 or produced by the U.S. Federal government or works licensed under the Creative Commons agreement, can be placed on reserve without consideration of Fair Use.'

In Canada, the end of 2008 witnessed a new pilot project that brought together different stakeholders in the copyright and publishing interests – Access Copyright (The Canadian Copyright Licensing Agency), Creative Commons Canada, Corp. and the Wikimedia Foundation – to form a Registry. According to the Creative Commons Website, found at *http:// creativecommons.ca/*, users will be able to use the Registry's integrated rights calculator to automatically determine each work's copyright status on an evolving basis. The Registry will also provide links to digital versions of the work and information about where a paper copy can be purchased, when available. Canada's library community was invited in 2008 to help test the Registry beta Website, an online, globally searchable catalogue of published Canadian literary works. These are developments that libraries should be aware of and take an active part in promotion or contribution.

Vendor acquisitions and mergers

Recent years have witnessed a number of significant changes in the integrated library systems (ILS) technology landscape – the mergers and acquisitions of vendors. Sirsi bought Dynix in 2005, forming the largest ILS vendor, with approximately 4,000 installations worldwide and over 20,000 library outlets. In 2006, SirsiDynix was acquired by Vista Equity Partners, found at *http://www.vistaequitypartners.com/*, a private equity firm focused on investing in software and technology-enabled businesses (Rogers, 2007). Ex Libris, found at *http://www.exlibrisgroup.com/category/Home*, a company that distributes DigiTool asset management, SFX scholarly linking, and Aleph integrated library systems, among other library technology, was acquired by Francisco Partners, found at *http://www.francisopartners.com*, a global private equity firm focused exclusively on investments in technology and technology-enabled services businesses, in the same year. Ex Libris and Francisco Partners completed acquisition of Endeavor Information Systems, an Elsevier company. The Cambridge Information Group (CIG) found at *http://www.cambridgeinformationgroup.com/*, a family-owned management and investment firm primarily focused on education, research and information services companies, acquired ProQuest Information and Learning to merge with its Cambridge Scientific Abstracts (CSA) unit to form ProQuest CSA. ProQuest, found at *http://www.proquest. com*, is a content provider and aggregator that offers such brands as CSA, UMI, Chadwyck-Healey, SIRS, and eLibrary.

One notable feature of these mergers and acquisitions is that the buyers are equity investors. Vista Equity Partners acquired SirsiDynix, Franciso Partners acquired Ex Libris and Endeavor. Both are private, tech-focused, equity firms that wanted to invest in virtual products beyond the ILS, like RFID (Radio-Frequency Identification), self-check, course management, etc. Indeed, as Clifford Lynch, Executive Director, CNI (Coalition for Networked Information) pointed out, 'the underlying conception of the ILS systems might be problem[atic] since it is very conflicted and flawed as we move into a digital world as opposed to describing and keeping track of physical artifacts' (Brown et al., 2007: 12). Digital content these days does not necessarily reside in the libraries or is not indexed in the ILS system. By looking at these underlying structural issues it explains why Google has become the preferred search engine for researchers. Libraries in the electronic age have been threatened by competition from other resources and service providers that target the same learner population – the students. Google was not aimed entirely at students but their impact on student behavior in searching for research materials has been so widely felt that libraries or database service providers are designing their search interfaces to mimic the core principle behind the Google logic – one search box supporting natural language searching.

Acquisitions and mergers also happen in the learning management systems industry. WebCT was launched commercially in 1997. In February 2006, WebCT was acquired by rival Blackboard Inc, a company founded in 1997 in the United States. Another U.S.-based system is Angel Learning Management Suite, which evolved from research conducted at Indiana University-Purdue University, Indianapolis and was marketed as a commercial application. In May 2009, Blackboard acquired Angel. A beneficial outcome of these merger and acquisition activities was that the vendors could then focus their energy on one platform instead of two parallel systems and have a larger pool of programmers to develop innovative products. SirsiDynix concentrated on developing a single platform based on Sirsi's Unicorn architecture instead of continued support and development of both Sirsi's Unicorn and Dynix's Horizon 8.x/Corinthian system. However, with tight library budgets, smaller institutions are finding it hard to continually shop around or move from one library system to another. At a recent e-reserve forum that took place in Ontario, Canada in June 2009, Seneca College described the time and energy they spent on product and data migration. They selected Endeavor's ENCompass, a digital management product which they liked, only to discover a couple of years later that as a result of the changes in Endeavor, the product was no longer supported. Their renewed efforts of using DigiTool, a digital asset management system created by Ex Libris (acquired by Francisco Partners, who also acquired Endeavor), were challenged by another change in direction of the vendor's development strategy.

In light of budgetary constraints, it is no surprise that libraries are beginning to take open-source systems more seriously. Speaking on 'Highlights of the Library and Information Technology Association (LITA) Top technology trends' at the American Library Association Midwinter 2007 meeting (Brown et al., 2007), Marshall Breeding from Vanderbilt University in the United States made reference to a major consortium in Georgia in the United States that developed an open source ILS called Evergreen, consisting of 252 small libraries. Clifford Lynch, who was on the same technology panel, was more skeptical of the open-source ILS movement, commenting on its cost and effectiveness in the long-run. Nevertheless, given the frequency of changes in the ILS market, the cost of migration between systems and budget constraints during harsh economic times, the appeal of adapting an open-source system to suit one's needs has increased considerably.

Conclusion

E-reserve has evolved over the years in many different ways, in response to changes in the library as well as the teaching and learning environment. The e-reserve delivery platform is usually a choice between access via the library catalogue and the integration with the institution's course management system. How to achieve that integration takes various shapes and forms. Some libraries manage to obtain the trust and consent of the faculty to provide a participatory role in merging the electronic readings into the course pages. Some succeed in creating a building block for importing library content into courses. Others develop their home-grown systems or modify on open-source software, while another group purchases commercially produced software designed to support the processing of faculty requests and copyright management procedures.

The problems faced by e-reserve operations in different countries may vary in scope and intensity. Copyright, however, is a universal concern. Legislation in many parts of the world seems to lag behind the forces of change in the digital environment, resulting in confusion of interpreting what is fair in copying and posting of electronic content.

Libraries themselves are facing the challenges of serving a user population that is very different from the previous generation. The paradigm of service philosophy has shifted from maintaining a physical facility for storage and dissemination of information to a hybrid of learning spaces that cater to both the demand for a physical facility for social interactions, study and research to a virtual cyberspace that attempts to blend in with the users' digital learning and recreational environment. Libraries are trying to keep pace with the trends for social networking, personalized learning, gaming, utmost mobility and flexibility and the insatiable demand for instant gratification of information needs of all kinds.

As well, libraries have to face competition from within the institution and from outside. To maintain their relevance and role in the educational process, librarians must work with their competitors and turn them into collaborators. Similar to the library, the institutions' information technology (IT) or the distance education (DE) departments are also looking for ways to best serve the users' interests, in providing the technology, the tools and the assistance needed for faculty to incorporate the various components of the teaching or learning processes into the information delivery platform. Faculty are instructed to develop their course shells and incorporate their assignments, testing and grading instruments and channels for communication with students into a one-stop shopping unit. The IT department or DE department often maintain the hardware and software, and have the largest programming support for keeping up a system for authenticating users, loading files (text or media) and tracking users' access. Externally, publishers, database aggregators, open access movements, and Web application developers are also competing for their share of the users' teaching and learning virtual space. Traditional publishers and database vendors create digital course packs or complementary learning guides to textbooks with quizzes, tests, tutorials and communication tools that resemble course management systems. Impatient with the cost and time associated with the copyright permission seeking process, faculty may increasingly be drawn to the open access and creative commons environment, bypassing the need for a library intermediary to create links to information resources. For those libraries or e-reserve operations that rely on digital asset management systems or other systems supporting the operations developed by commercial enterprises, the frequent mergers and acquisitions in the vendors' world, resulting in a migration of data and re-training of staff and users, is a huge challenge to the library budget, staff resources and user education initiatives.

The library literature searches, surveys conducted and opinions expressed at conferences or workshops indicate that there is no single e-reserve system that can fit all sizes of institutions and their wants. The authors discovered in their 2008 survey of 57 e-reserve operations, mainly in North America (Appendix I), that there were almost as many libraries using one e-reserve system (52%) as more than one system (43%). There were at least 22 different combinations of e-reserve systems used. There is no best practice that can be universally applied. From the wide array of approaches mentioned above, libraries have to choose the system that is most relevant and applicable to their own environments. Based on their research, however, the authors hypothesize that integration of e-reserve into the course management system may well evolve as the most widely used model. The strategies described in this book represent the collective wisdom of libraries that have been faced with similar challenges. Hopefully, one can learn from the shortcomings of these experiences, and build on their successes to create, as needed, other new approaches to e-reserve in the ever changing world of digital information and learning management.

Appendix I

Ryerson University Library December 2008 Survey of E-Reserve Operations – Results Summary

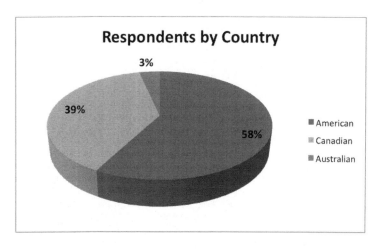

Only 1 of the 57 respondents did not offer e-reserve service

E-reserve system findings

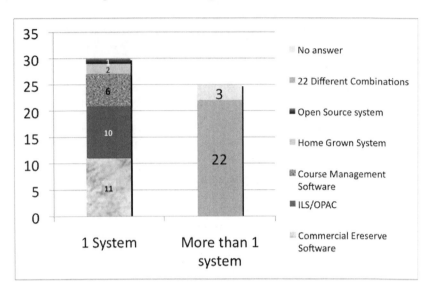

'Other' access modes

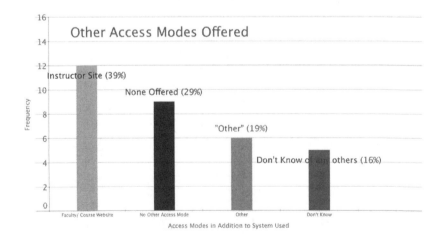

Formats provided in E-reserve

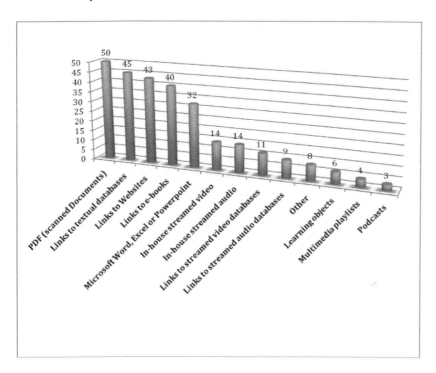

Owned vs. not owned materials

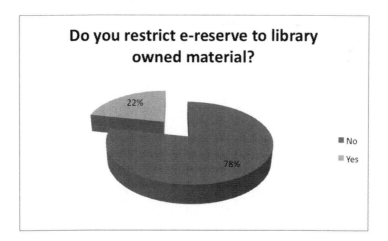

Types of not owned materials include:

- linking to anything as long as copyright is OK
- external Websites/publicly accessible materials
- faculty materials (lecture notes, etc.)
- student-created materials.

Collaboration

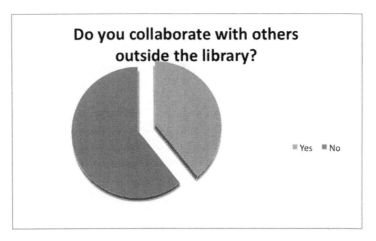

Partners are generally Distance Education and IT.

Copyright permissions

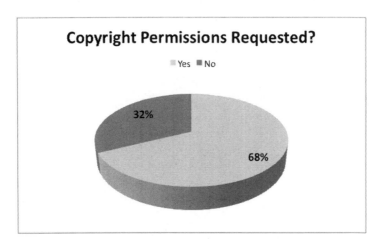

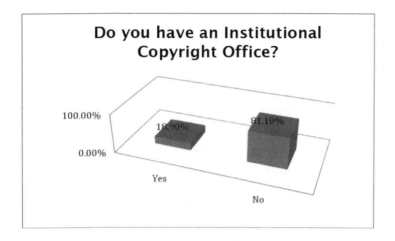

Do you have an Institutional Copyright Office?

100.00%

0.00%

18.90%

81.10%

Yes

No

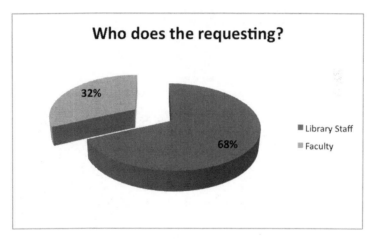

Who does the requesting?

32%

68%

Library Staff

Faculty

Request tracking

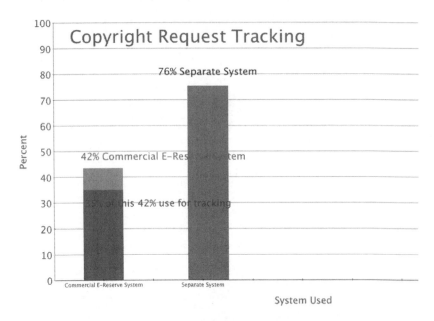

41.8% use a commercial e-reserve system, but only 35% use it to track copyright requests Separate systems to track copyright include a variety of methods including Excel, Google Docs, manually and others.

Promotion methods

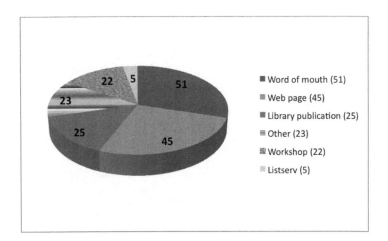

Evaluation methods

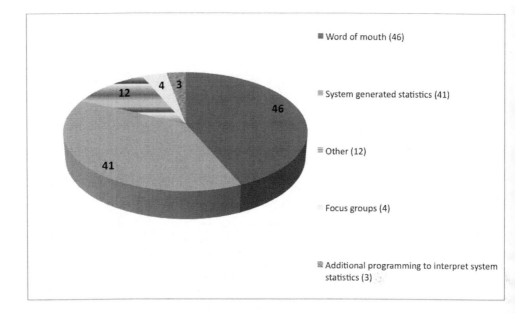

- Word of mouth (46)
- System generated statistics (41)
- Other (12)
- Focus groups (4)
- Additional programming to interpret system statistics (3)

Appendix II

*Ryerson University Library Faculty
Survey on Reserve Services
(May, 2005)*

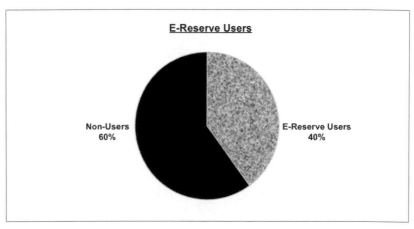

E-Reserve Users

Non-Users
60%

E-Reserve Users
40%

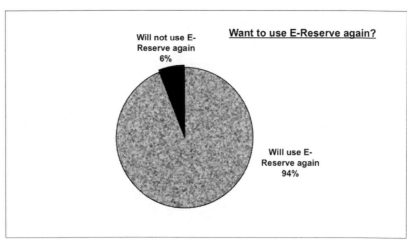

Will not use E-
Reserve again
6%

Want to use E-Reserve again?

Will use E-
Reserve again
94%

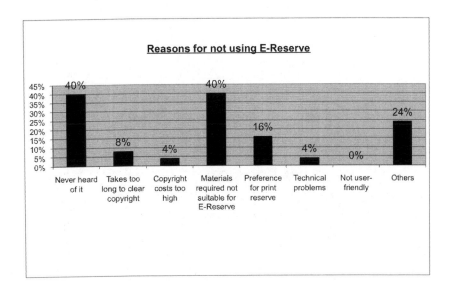

Reasons for not using E-Reserve

Appendix III

Ryerson University Library Faculty
Requests for Reserve Services
(2003–5)

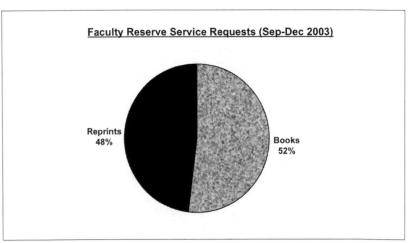

Faculty Reserve Service Requests (Sep-Dec 2003)

Reprints
48%

Books
52%

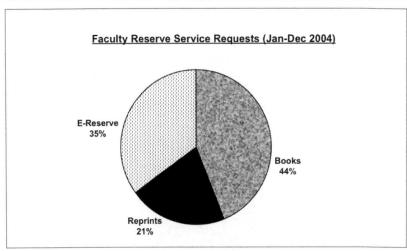

Faculty Reserve Service Requests (Jan-Dec 2004)

E-Reserve
35%

Books
44%

Reprints
21%

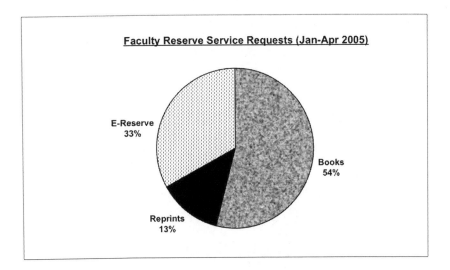

Faculty Reserve Service Requests (Jan-Apr 2005)

E-Reserve 33%

Books 54%

Reprints 13%

Appendix IV

Ryerson University Library Student Survey on E-Reserve in Blackboard (Spring/Summer 2006)

1. How do you access E-Reserve materials in Blackboard? (You may choose more than one answer)

From library computer	2
From other computer on campus	0
From work computer	12
From home computer	17
From your portable computer (e.g. laptop, palmtop)	5
Total respondents	22

2. During this term have you had any problems seeing the full-text of an article on E-Reserve?

Never	10
1–5 times	12
6–10 times	0
More than 10 times	0
Total respondents	22

3. Course readings can be provided in a number of ways. Please select the one you prefer.

Print course packs sold at the University Bookstore or mailed to your address at a cost	2
Short-term loans (2 or 24 hours) for you to request at the Library Circulation desk	0
Links to electronic materials posted to E-Reserve within your Blackboard course	20
Total respondents	22

Comments on E-Reserve in Blackboard:

1. I did appreciate the fact that the readings were available on e-reserve that saved me and other students a lot of money. Despite the few times that it did not show properly, it was pretty easy to use.

2. A very helpful and convenient model.

3. I really enjoyed using E-Reserve because it gave me the option of doing the readings on the computer or printing out a hard copy. And it was fantastic that I didn't have to spend more money on another textbook I would never use again.

4. Like it a lot!

5. It's overall very user friendly and convenient.

6. Listings are alphabetical by title – author would be better.

Appendix V

Ryerson University Library Distance Education Student Surveys (2007)

March 2007 Survey Results (all courses and 863 respondents):

1. Have you had any problems seeing full text of an article on E-Reserve?

Never	22%
1–5 times	15%
6–10 times	1%
Not applicable	59%

2. Have you had any problems viewing streaming videos on E-reserve?

Never	15%
1–5 times	5%
6–10 times	1%
Not applicable	78%

November 2007 Survey Results (all courses and 833 respondents):

1. Did you find it easy to locate E-Reserve readings within the Blackboard course home page?

Yes	28%
No	9%
Never used E-Reserve	61%
No answer	2%

2. How many times you had problems opening up an article link or seeing a full-text article on E-Reserve?

Never	19%
1–5 times	17%
6–10 times	3%
Never used E-Reserve	55%
No answer	3%

References

A shot heard round the academic world: Harvard FAS mandates open access (2008, February 14). *Library Journal Academic Newswire.* Retrieved October 19, 2009 from *http://www.libraryjournal.com/info/CA6532658.html#news1*

Albanese, A. (2008, May 15). Georgia State sued over e-reserves. *Library Journal, 133*(9), 16–17.

Apple, Inc. (2008). Apple education – iTunes U user's guide. Retrieved from *http://deimos.apple.com/rsrc/doc/AppleEducation-iTunes UUsersGuide/Introduction/chapter_1_section_1.html*

Apple, Inc. (2009). Mobile learning and iTunes U: Think outside the classroom. Retrieved from *http://www.apple.com/ca/education/mobile-learning/*

Apple, Inc. (2010). iTunes U. Retrieved from *http://www.apple.com/education/mobile-learning/*

Ariew, S. (2008). YouTube culture and the academic library: A guide to online open access educational videos. *Choice: Current Reviews for Academic Libraries, 45*(12), 2057–2063.

Ashling, J. (2008). Universities and libraries thrive on Earth and Mars. *Information Today, 25*(7), 22–23.

Association of Research Libraries (2009). *The Research library's role in digital repository services: Final report of the ARL Digital Repository Issues Task Force.* Retrieved from *http://www.arl.org/bm~doc/repository-services-report.pdf*

Austerberry, D. (2005). *The technology of video and audio streaming* (2nd ed.). Burlington, MA: Focal Press.

Austin, B. (2002). A brief history of electronic reserves. *Journal of Interlibrary Loan, Document Delivery & Information Supply, 12*(2), 1–15. doi: 10.1300/J110v12n02_01

Austin, B., & Taylor, K. (2003). Four scenarios concerning fair use and copyright costs: Electronic reserves at the University of Colorado, Boulder. *Journal of Interlibrary Loan, Document Delivery & Information Supply, 13*(3), 1–13. doi: 10.1300/J110v13n03_01

Austin, B., & Taylor, K. (2007). Assessment of electronic reserves services at the University of Colorado, Boulder. *Journal of Interlibrary Loan, Document Delivery & Electronic Reserve, 17*(1), 83–95. doi: 10.1300/J474v17n01_10

Bell, S. J., & Krasulski, M. J. (2004). Electronic reserves, library databases and courseware: A complementary relationship. *Journal of Interlibrary Loan, Document Delivery & Electronic Reserve, 15*(1), 75–85. doi: 10.1300/J474v15n01_07

Bennett, S., Maton, K., & Kervin, L. (2008). The 'digital natives' debate: A critical review of the evidence. *British Journal of Educational Technology, 39*(5), 775–786. doi:10.1111/j.1467–8535.2007.00793.x

Black, E. L. (2008). Toolkit approach to integrating library resources into the learning management system. *The Journal of Academic Librarianship, 34*(6), 496–501. *http://journals2.scholarsportal.info.ezproxy.lib.ryerson.ca/tmp/ 6767349297226825003.pdf*

Blackboard Inc. (1997–2010). Vanderbilt iTunes U building block. Retrieved from *http://www.blackboard.com/Support/Extensions/Extension-Details.aspx? ExtensionID=23001*

Bridges, A. (2007). E-reserves threatened at Cornell. *College & Research Libraries News, 68*(5), 317.

Bridgewater, R. (2008). Shifting responsibility for electronic reserves copyright permissions from the academic departments to the library: From confusion to cooperation. *Journal of Interlibrary Loan, Document Delivery & Electronic Reserve, 18*(2), 141–152. doi: 10.1300/10723030802098840

Brown, J. S. (2000). Growing up digital: how the web changes work, education, and the ways people learn. *Change, 32*(2), 10–20.

Brown, M., Cox, C., Gelfand, J., & Riggs, C. (2007). Reports from the American Association Midwinter Meeting, Seattle, Washington January 18–22, 2007. Highlights of the Library and Information Technology Association (LITA) top technology trends. *Library Hi Tech News, 24*(3), 7–12.

Burich, N. J., & Rholes, J. (2004). Developing partnerships to create electronic reserves at the University of Kansas Libraries. *Journal of Access Services, 1*(4), 59–70. doi: 10.1300/J204v01n04_04

Calsada, M. (2006). Ares-automating reserves: An overview from the developer. *Journal of Interlibrary Loan, Document Delivery & Electronic Reserve, 16*(3), 21–25. doi: 10.1300/J474v16n03_04

Carlson, S. (2005, April 22). Legal battle brews over availability of texts on online reserve at U. of California library. *The Chronicle of Higher Education, 51*(33), p. A36.

Chen, H. L., & Choi, G. (2005). Construction of a digital video library: A socio-technical pilot study on college students' attitudes. *The Journal of Academic Librarianship, 31*(5), 469–476.

Cheung, O., & Patrick, S. (2007). E-Reserve in Blackboard: Chalk it up to collaboration. *Journal of Interlibrary Loan, Document Supply & Electronic Reserve, 17*(3), 129–143. doi: 10.1300/J474v17n03_16

Colebatch, C. (2008, August). *Crown copyright and the privatization of information.* Paper session presented at the International Federation of Library Associations (IFLA) Conference, Quebec, Canada. Retrieved from *http:// www.ifla.org/IV/ifla74/papers/087-Colebatch-en.pdf*

Collis, B., & De Boer, W. (2004). E-learning by design: Teachers as learners: Embedded tools for implementing a CMS. *TechTrends, 48*(6), 7–12. doi: 10.1007/BF0276357

Cox, D. (2009). Are digital textbooks the money-saving wave of the future? Retrieved from *http://www.dailytitan.com/2009/08/are-digital-textbooks-the-money-saving-wave-of-the-future/*

Crow, R. (2002). The case for institutional repositories: a SPARC position paper. *ARL Bimonthly Report* 223, 1–37. Retrieved from *http://works.bepress.com/ir_research/7/*

Cubbage, C. (2003). Electronic reserves and Blackboard's course management system. *Journal of Interlibrary Loan, Document Delivery & Information Supply*, *13*(4), 21–32. doi: 10.1300/J110v13n04_04

Cubbage, C. (2007). The changing cost environment of managing copyright for electronic reserves. *Journal of Interlibrary Loan, Document Delivery & Electronic Reserve*, *18*(1), 57–66. doi: 10.1300/J474v18n01_07

Dalton, J. T. (2007). Electronic reserves and the copyright challenge in Canada. *Journal of Interlibrary Loan, Document Delivery & Electronic Reserve*, *17*(1), 97–120. doi: 10.1300/J474v17n01_11

De Rosa, C., Cantrell, J., Hawk, J., & Wilson, A. (2006). *College students' perceptions of libraries and information resources: A report to the OCLC membership.* Retrieved from *http://www.oclc.org/reports/pdfs/studentperceptions.pdf*

Dekker, J. (2009). Beyond YouTube: Sources for online video. *Access 15*(4), 32–3.

Dun, J. & Hollar, S. (2008). *Integrating licensed library resources with Sakai final narrative report: January 1, 2006 – June 30, 2008.* Retrieved from *http://confluence.sakaiproject.org/download/attachments/9895942/Sakaibrary-finalreport.pdf*

ENCompass installed at 17 institutions (2002, February 2). *Information Today*. Retrieved October 19, 2009. from *http://www.infotoday.com/IT/feb02/news20.htm*

Eng, S., & Hernandez, F. A. (2006). Managing streaming video: A new role for technical services. *Library Collections, Acquisitions and Technical Services*, *30*(3–4), 214–223.

Ferster, A., Lamont, S., Leonard, W., McCulloch, A., Rahman, S., & Smith, A. (2006). *University of Waterloo library report: Faculty perspectives on reserves.* Retrieved from *http://www.lib.uwaterloo.ca/News/UWLibDocs/reservereport.html*

57 College Presidents declare support for legislation to ensure public access to publicly funded research in the U.S. (2009, September 23). *Alliance for Taxpayer Access*. Retrieved October 19, 2009 from *http://www.taxpayeraccess.org/news/news_releases/09–0923.shtml*

Frand, J. (2000). The information-age mindset: Changes in students and implications for higher education. *Educause Review*, *35*(5), 15–24. Retrieved from *http://net.educause.edu/ir/library/pdf/ERM0051.pdf*

Gerlich, B. K., & Perrier, A. (2003). Arts Instruction in the age of technology: Providing library services to support studio and survey faculty who use technology for instruction. *Information Technology and Libraries*, *22*(2), 79–83.

Gibbs, J. (2009). Doing it yourself: Coventry university library's streaming project. *Art Libraries Journal*, *34*(3), 21–25.

Gross, M., & Latham, D. (2009). Undergraduate perceptions of information literacy: Defining, attaining, and self-assessing skills. *College & Research Libraries*, *70*(4), 336–350.

Grotophorst, W., & Frumkin, J. (2002). OSCR: Open source software and electronic reserves. In J. Rosedale (Ed.), *Managing electronic reserves* (pp. 93–108). Chicago, IL: American Library Association.

Groves, P. (2009). *Making required readings available to students.* Retrieved from *http://www.lib.sfu.ca/my-library/services-for-you/required-readings*

Hafner, K. (2008, April 16). Publishers sue Georgia State on digital reading matter. *The New York Times.* Retrieved from *http://www.nytimes.com/2008/04/16/technology/16school.html?_r=1&ref=business*

Hanna, D. E. (2003). Building a leadership vision: Eleven strategic challenges for higher education, *Educause Review, 38*(4), 25–34.

Hersey, D. P. (2005). The future of access services: Should there be one? *Journal of Access Services, 2*(4), 1–6.

Hiller, B. (2004). Docutek's ERes electronic reserve software: An evaluation. *Journal of Interlibrary Loan, Document Delivery & Electronic Reserve, 15*(1), 99–118. doi: 10.1300/J474v15n01_09

Horava, T. (2009, January). *Copyright communication in academic libraries* [PowerPoint slides]. Retrieved from *http://www.accessola.com/superconference2009/showSession.php?lsession=1803&usession=1803*

Indiana University Digital Library Program (2008). *Sakaibrary: Integrating licensed library resources with Sakai.* Retrieved from *http://www.dlib.indiana.edu/projects/sakai/index.shtml*

Innerd, C. (2009). *How to share citations using RefShare.*Retrieved from *http://inkandelectrons.blogspot.com/2009/05/how-to-share-citations-using-refshare.html*

Jankowska, M. A. (2004). Identifying university professors' information needs in the challenging environment of information and communication technologies. *Journal of Academic Librarianship, 30*(1), 51–66.

Kesten, P. R. (2002). Perspectives of an enlightened vendor. In J. Rosedale (Ed.), *Managing electronic reserves* (pp. 148–167). Chicago, IL: American Library Association.

Kimball, S. J. (2010). *Collaborating with IT to deliver e-reserves using Drupal and Zotero.* [PowerPoint slides]. Retrieved from *http://electroniclibrarian.com/erlwiki/cgi_img_auth.php5/5/5c/TUE_105_Collaborating_with_IT_to_Deliver_E-Reserves.ppt.*

Kristof, C. (1999). *Electronic reserves operation in ARL libraries, SPEC Flyer 245, May 1999.* Retrieved August 28, 2009, from *http://www.arl.org/bm~doc/spec245web.pdf*

Kuh, G. D., & Gonyea, R. M. (2003). The role of the academic library in promoting student engagement in learning. *College & Research Libraries, 64*(4), 256–282.

Leonard, W., McCulloch, A., Lamont, S., & Townsend, A. (2006). *University of Waterloo library report: Student perspectives on reserves.* Retrieved from *http://www.lib.uwaterloo.ca/News/UWLibDocs/student_perspectives_reserves.html*

Lu, S. (2001). A model for choosing an electronic reserves system: A pre-implementation study at the Library of Long Island University's Brooklyn campus. *Journal of Interlibrary Loan, Document Delivery & Information Supply, 12*(2), 25–44. doi: 10.1300/J110v12n02_03

Lynch, C. A. (2003). Institutional repositories: Essential infrastructure for scholarship in the digital age. *ARL: A Bimonthly Report, 226,* 1–7. Retrieved from *http://www.arl.org/resources/pubs/br/br226/br226ir.shtml*

Lynch, C. A., & Lippincott, J. K. (2005). Institutional repository deployment in the United States as of early 2005. *D-Lib Magazine, 11*(9). Retrieved from *http://www.dlib.org/dlib/september05/lynch/09lynch.html*

McCarthy, G., Banerjee, S., & Wilson, S. (2008). *Is your library website enough?* Poster session presented at the International Federation of Library Associations (IFLA) Conference, Quebec, Canada.

McGinnis, L. (2000). Bringing order out of chaos: The challenge of managing e-reserves copyright permissions. *Journal of Interlibrary Loan & Information Supply, 11*(2), 39–50. doi: 10.1300/J110v11n02_04

McLean, N., & Lynch, C. (2004). *Interoperability between library information services and learning environments – bridging the gaps: A joint white paper on behalf of the IMS Global Learning Consortium and the Coalition for Networked Information.* Retrieved from *http://www.estandard.no/tilgjengelig/CNIandIMS_2004.pdf*

Meikle, S., & Vine, R. (2008, June). *Matching courses to resources: Automating the integration of discipline-specific library resources in Blackboard courses* [Abstract]. Poster session presented at the 27th Annual American Library Association Conference, Anaheim, California, United States. Retrieved August 22, 2009, from *http://www.lib.jmu.edu/org/ala/abstracts/2008/default.aspx#200*

Melamut, S. J., Thibodeau, P. L., & Albright, E. D. (2000). Fair use or not fair use: That is the electronic reserves question. *Journal of Interlibrary Loan, Document Delivery & Information Supply, 11*(1), 3–28. doi: 10.1300/J110v11n01_02

Michel, J. P., Hurst, S., & Revelle, A. (2009). Vodcasting, iTunes U, and faculty collaboration. *Electronic Journal of Academic & Special Librarianship, 10*(1), 6.

Morrison, H. (2009, September 30). Re: Dramatic growth of open access [Web log message]. Retrieved October 19, 2009 from *http://poeticeconomics.blogspot.com*

Neumayr, T., & Monaghn, C. (2007). *100 million iPods sold.* Retrieved from *http://www.apple.com/pr/library/2007/04/09ipod.html*

Noel, W. (2005). *Copyright matters: Some key questions and answers for teachers* (2nd ed.). Retrieved from *http://www.cmec.ca/Publications/Lists/Publications/Attachments/12/copyrightmatters.pdf*

Oblinger, D. (2003). Boomers & gen-xers, millennials: Understanding the 'new students'. *Educause Review, 38*(4), 37–44. Retrieved from *http://net.educause.edu/ir/library/pdf/erm0342.pdf*

OCLC Online Computer Library Center, Inc. (n.d.). *PURL.* Retrieved from *http://purl.org/docs/index.html*

OCLC Online Computer Library Center, Inc. E-Learning Task Force (2003). *Libraries and the enhancement of e-learning.* Retrieved from *http://www5.oclc.org/downloads/community/elearning.pdf*

OCLC Online Computer Library Center, Inc. (2009) *EZproxy® authentication and access software at a glance.* Retrieved from *http://www.oclc.org/ezproxy/about/default.htm*

O'Hara, E. (2006). Eliminating e-reserves: One library's experience. *Technical Services Quarterly, 24*(2), 35–43.

Paskin, N. (2010). Digital object identifier (DOI) system. In M. J. Bates & M. N. Maack (Eds.). *Encyclopedia of Library and Information Sciences* (3rd ed.). doi: 10.1081/E-ELIS3-120044418

Pearce, L. (2001). Lessons learned: The development of electronic reserves at the University of Calgary. *D-Lib Magazine, 7*(11). Retrieved from *http://www.dlib.org/dlib/november01/pearce/11pearce.html*

Peters-Lise, J. (2009) *Transitioning to DigiTool for e-reserves* [PowerPoint slides]. Retrieved from *http://lib.guelphhumber.ca/resources/documents/DigiTool_JenniferPeters-Lise_Seneca.pdf*

Peters-Lise, J., Lam, C., Buczinski, J., Darmohusodo, Y., Foo, J., Hoyle, L. et al. (2006). *Canadian E-reserves environmental scan summary report.* Retrieved from *http://74.125.95.132/search?q=cache:fv30peNyfMkJ:people.senecac.on.ca/jennifer.peters-lise/Can_E-res_Scan_Report.pdf+seneca+e-reserves+environment+scan&hl=en&ct=clnk&cd=1&gl=ca*

Pinfield, S. (2003). Open archives and UK institutions. *D-Lib Magazine, 9*(3). Retrieved from *http://www.dlib.org/dlib/march03/pinfield/03pinfield.html*

Poe, J. (2006). Marketing electronic reserves at a university library: Start spreading the news. *Journal of Interlibrary Loan, Document Delivery & Electronic Reserve, 16*(4), 93–102. doi: 10.1300/J474v16n04_10

Poe, J., & McAbee, S. (2008), Electronic reserves, copyright, and CMS integration – six years later. *Journal of Access Services, 5*(1/2), 251–263. doi: 10.1080/15367960802198879

Poe, J., & Skaggs, B. (2007). Course reserves: Using Blackboard for e-reserves delivery. *Journal of Interlibrary Loan, Document Delivery & Electronic Reserve, 18*(1), 79–91. doi: 10.1300/J474v18n01_09

Poleykett, B. (2003). *Managing Australian electronic reserves* [Memorandum]. Retrieved from *http://www.caul.edu.au/surveys/Managing_eReserves2003.doc*

Poleykett, B., & Benn, J. (2003). *Beyond e-reserve: Implementation of a repository-based reading list management system at the University of Western Australia.* Retrieved from *http://www.caudit.edu.au/educauseaustralasia07/authors_papers/Poleykett-109%20FINAL.pdf*

Potocki, J. (2006). *Effective practice: iPods + iTunes + faculty = iTunes U at Fairfield University.* Retrieved from *http://net.educause.edu/ir/library/pdf/EPS291.pdf*

Pritchard, T. (2009). *University students turn to downloadable textbooks as a way to save money.* Retrieved from *http://www.google.com/hostednews/canadianpress/article/ALeqM5iMGul4KISC7lmbM3wE1w7Z4eVb0A*

Prosser, H. G. (2006). Video streaming in the Wild West. *Partnership: The Canadian Journal of Library & Information Practice & Research, 1*(1), 1–9.

Raines, C. (2002). Managing millenials. In *Connecting generations: The sourcebook for a new workplace.* Retrieved from *http://www.generationsatwork.com/articles_millenials.php*

RefWorks-COS (2009a). *RefWorks home page.* Retrieved from *www.refworks.com*

RefWorks-COS (2009b). Blackboard. In *Help – RefWorks home page.* Retrieved from *https://www.refworks.com/refworks/help/Blackboard.htm*

RefWorks-COS (2009c). Converting from other bibliographic management programs. In *Help – RefWorks home page.* Retrieved from *http://www.refworks.com/RefWorks/help/Exporting_from_Bibliographic_Programs_and_Importing_into_RefWorks.htm*

RefWorks-COS (2009d). Using the output style editor. In *Help – RefWorks home page*. Retrieved from *http://www.refworks.com/RefWorks/help/Using_the_Output_Format_Editor2.htm*

Rice, L. (2006, October 3). C.U. changes e-reserve policy to avoid lawsuit. *The Cornell Daily Sun*. Retrieved from *http://cornellsun.com/node/18733*

Rieger, O. Y., Horne, A. K., & Revels, I. (2004). Linking course web sites to library collections and services. *The Journal of Academic Librarianship, 30*(3), 205–211.

Rogers, M. (2007). Vista equity partners buys SirsiDynix. *Library Journal, 132*(2), 25.

Roig, M. (1997). Can undergraduate students determine whether text has been plagiarized? *Psychological Record, 47*(1), 113–122.

Rosedale, J. (Ed.) (2002). *Managing electronic reserves*. Chicago IL: American Library Association.

Run Run Shaw Library, City University of Hong Kong (2007). *Building reading lists linkable from Blackboard course sites with RefWorks*. Retrieved from *http://www.cityu.edu.hk/lib/instruct/webteach/rwbb/rwlink_intro.htm*.

Schmidt, S. J. (2002). Staffing issues for electronic reserves. In J. Rosedale (Ed.), *Managing electronic reserves* (pp. 21–28). Chicago, IL: American Library Association.

Shearer, K. (2006). The CARL institutional repositories project: A collaborative approach to addressing the challenges of IRs in Canada. *Library Hi Tech, 24*(2), 165–172.

Shephard, K. (2003). Questioning, promoting and evaluating the use of streaming video to support student learning. *British Journal of Educational Technology, 34*(3), 295–308.

Sinclair, G. (2009). Bypassing or supplementing OpenURL via title links in RefWorks.In *SPOT-DOCS – the collaborative documentation portal for Scholars Portal*. Retrieved from *http://spotdocs.scholarsportal.info/display/sfxdocs/Bypassing+or+supplementing+OpenURL+via+title+links+in+RefWorks*

Song, Y., Nixon, C., & Burmood, J. (2001). Video streaming applications: QuickTime, Real, and Windows Media. *Internet Librarian 2001: Collected Presentations*, 222–231.

Suber, P. (2004). *A very brief introduction to open access*. Retrieved from *http://earlham.edu/~peters/fos/brief.htm*

Swan, A. (2008). The business of digital repositories. In K. Weenink, L. Waaijers & K. van Godtsenhoven (Eds.), *A DRIVER's guide to European repositories* (pp. 1–41). Amsterdam: Amsterdam University Press. Retrieved from *http://eprints.ecs.soton.ac.uk/14455/*

Thomas, D. (2007a). *RefWorks: Easy as 1,2,3*. Retrieved from *http://www.ryerson.ca/library/info/databases/refworks/refworks123/RefWorks_easy_as_1_2_3.html*

Thomas, D. (2007b). *RefShare: Easy as 1,2,3*. Retrieved from *http://www.ryerson.ca/library/info/databases/refworks/refshare/RefShare%20Blackboard.html*

Thomas, J. (2004). Digital video, the final frontier. *Library Journal (1976)*, 8–10.

Tolwinska, A. (2009, August 24). CrossRef indicators. [Web log message]. Retrieved from *http://www.crossref.org/crweblog/2009/08/crossref_indicators_118.html*

Valentine, D. (2009). *E-texts roil market.* Retrieved September 1, 2009, from *http://www.dailyiowan.com/2009/09/01/Metro/12588.html*

Walton, L. (2009). *Refworks at the Steacie Library York University* [PDF document]. Retrieved from *http://lib.guelphhumber.ca/resources/documents/refworks_laurawalton_york.pdf*

Warren, S. A. (2005). DOIs and deeplinked e-reserves: Innovative links for the future. *Technical Services Quarterly, 22*(4), 1–17. doi: 10.1300/J124v22n04_01

Wills, S. (2004). *AUCC Notes for a presentation to the House of Commons Standing Committee on Canadian Heritage regarding the Government Status Report on Copyright Reform: Access Issues Technology Enhanced Learning April 28, 2004.* Retrieved February 17, 2010 from *http://docs.google.com/viewer?a=v&q=cache:I9DKCz_-vMUJ:www.aucc.ca/_pdf/english/reports/2004/copyright_04_28_e.pdf+wills+AUCC+speaking otes+house+of+commons+copyright+reform&hl=en&gl=ca&sig=AHIEtbRWPxPSEL8-rJhCdcV8-vXF4Q9Jnw*

Wills, S. (2009). *AUCC Speaking notes roundtable on Copyright Reform July 29, 2009.* Retrieved from *http://www.aucc.ca/_pdf/english/reports/2009/copyright_reform_07_29_e.pdf*

Wilson, S. (2009). The future is here: Library services for mobile devices. *Access, 15*(4), 18–19.

Wynstra, J. (2005). Creating, designing, and building an electronic reserve system. *Journal of Interlibrary Loan, Document Delivery & Electronic Reserve, 15*(4), 57–81. doi: 10.1300/J474v15n04_06

Young, J. (2009, February 12). Re: Cdigix ceases operations, citing poor economy. [Web log message]. Retrieved from *http://chronicle.com/blogPost/Cdigix-Ceases-Operations/4528/*

Further reading

Abram, S. (2006).Islands in the stream. *Information Outlook, 10*(7), 38.

Add video to course reserves at the library (2007). *Library Journal, 132*(6), 13.

Austin, B. (2005). The futures of course reserves. *Journal of Interlibrary Loan, Document Delivery & Electronic Reserve, 15*(2), 43–50. doi: 10.1300/J474v15n02_07

Bayne, P. S., & Hodge, C. (2001). Digital audio reserves: A collaborative project at the University of Tennessee. *Journal of Interlibrary Loan, Document Delivery & Information Supply, 11*(4), 25–36. doi: 10.1300/J110v11n04_02

Chen, L., Mills, J., & Ma, Y. (2001). Electronic reserves using VOYAGER. *Georgia Library Quarterly, 38*(3), 14–16.

Chrisfield, T. (1999). La Trobe university library video on demand services trial. *Multimedia Information and Technology, 25*(2), 143–147.

Jonas-Dwyer, D., & Pospisil, R. (2004). The millennial effect: Implications for academic development. In *Transforming knowledge into wisdom, proceedings of the 27th HERDSA annual conference* (pp. 194–207). Retrieved from *http://www.herdsa.org.au/newsite/wp/wp-content/uploads/conference/2004/PDF/P050-jt.pdf*

Lamb, A., & Johnson, L. (2007). Podcasting in the school library, part 1: Integrating podcasts and vodcasts into teaching and learning. *Teacher Librarian*, *34*(3), 54.

Li, J., Runderson, R. A., Burnham, J. F., Staggs, G. B., Robertson, J. C., & Williams, T. L. (2005). Delivering distance training to rural health care professionals. *Medical Reference Services Quarterly*, *24*(1), 41–54.

McCloskey, J. (2002). Electronic reserves in support of online learning communities: Report on a pilot project at Widener University. *Journal of Access Services*, *1*(2), 15–23.

McDonald, R. H., & Thomas, C. (2006). Disconnects between library culture and millennial generation values. *Educause Quarterly*, *29*(4), 4–6.

New digital resource sharing service lets libraries add free download media (2007). *Public Libraries*, *46*(6), 70.

Pace, A. K. (2007). *What the FUD? Whose system is this, anyway?* Retrieved August 20, 2009, from *http://www.ala.org/ala/alonline/techspeaking/2007columns/ALA_print_layout_1_378920_378920.cfm*

Soete, G. (1996). Issues and innovations in electronic reserves. In *Association of Research Libraries: Transforming libraries* (Issue 1). Retrieved January 9, 2009, from *http://www.arl.org/transform/eres/eres.html*

Tiessen, R. (2007). Copyright's effect on interlibrary loan in Canada and the United States. *Journal of Interlibrary Loan, Document Delivery & Electronic Reserve*, *18*(1), 101–111. doi: 10.1300/J474v18n01_11

Walchak, S. B. (2007). Electronic reserves at Fort Lewis College using Innovative Interfaces, Millennium integrated library system. *Journal of Interlibrary Loan, Document Delivery & Electronic Reserve*, *17*(1), 165–181. doi: 10.1300/J474v17n01_15

Wilkinson, M. A. (2009, January). *Changes to Canada's Copyright Act* [PowerPoint slides]. Retrieved from *http://www.accessola.com/superconference2009/showSession.php?lsession=1001&usession=1001*

Wilson S. & McCarthy, G. (2010). The mobile university: from the library to the campus. *Reference Services Review*, *38*(2), 214–232, doi: 10.1108/00907321011044990

Ziegenfuss, D. H., & McCloskey, J. M. (2004). A consideration of Docutek's electronic reserve system in a university's courseware environment. *Journal of Interlibrary Loan, Document Delivery & Electronic Reserve*, *15*(1), 87–97. doi: 10.1300/J474v15n01_08

Index